Poetry

A Thanksgiving Eclogue (1954)
The Precisions (1955)
The Responses (1956)
Stances and Distances (1957)
The Marches (1957)
A Table in Provence (1959)
The Descent from Daimonji (1959)
Clocked Stone (1959)
For Sure (1959)
For Instance (1962)
Sun Rock Man (1962)
In No Time (1963)
For Good (1964)
In Good Time (1964)
All in All (1965)
Nonce (1965)
For You (1966)
Stead (1966)
For Granted (1967)
Words for Each Other (1967)
& Without End (1968)
No Less (1968)
Hearth (1968)
No More (1969)
Plight (1969)
Nigh (1970)
Livingdying (1970)
Of the Breath of (1970)
For Keeps (1970)
For Now (1971)
Out and Out (1972)
Be Quest (1972)
A Language Without Words (1973)
So Far (1973)
Poems: Thanks to Zuckerkandl (1973)
Three Poems (1973)
O/I (1974)
RSVP (1974)
Yet (1974)
For Dear Life (1975)

Prose

At: Bottom (1966)
The Act of Poetry (1976)
William Bronk: An Essay (1976)

Translations

Cool Melon (Basho) (1959)
Cool Gong (1959)
Selected Frogs (Shimpei Kusano) (1963)
Back Roads to Far Towns (Basho) (1968)
Frogs and Others: Poems (Shimpei Kusano) (1969)
Things (Francis Ponge) (1971)
Leaves of Hypnos (René Char) (1973)
Breathings (Philippe Jaccottet) (1974)

VOLUME I

CID CORMAN

WORD for WORD

ESSAYS
ON
THE ARTS
OF
LANGUAGE

BLACK SPARROW PRESS / SANTA BARBARA / 1977

ACKNOWLEDGEMENTS

My thanks are here offered the various editors of the magazines in which, as indicated, most of these essays, often slightly revised now, originally appeared.

My thanks also to the Chapelbrook Foundation for extended support.

LIBRARY OF CONGRESS CATALOGING IN PUBLICATION DATA

Corman, Cid.
   Word for word: Essays on the arts of language, vol. I.

   1. Literature—collected works.   I. Title.
PN37.C6   809   76-48282
ISBN 0-87685-275-4 (paper back)
ISBN 0-87685-276-2 (trade cloth)
ISBN 0-87685-277-0 (signed cloth)

for Clayton

". . . I speak as my understanding
instructs me, and as mine honesty
puts it to utterance."

TABLE OF CONTENTS

These essays were not intended to be collected. They were written invariably for the sake of something that moved me and I thought might be shared or at least made known to others who might also be moved.

Judgment has seemed to me for a long time now only a way of pointing back at the judge, who may choose to hide behind the mask of principle. And to the extent that judgment intrudes here you must look to my eyes to see what comes through anyhow.

Many of the pieces are in a sense open letters, addressed as much to poets who are friends and whom I cherish, beyond all critique.

There is an effort throughout to forget all alleged hierarchies, to avoid jargon of any kind, and to let the work evoked appear in its fulness.

If the essays provoke thought and feeling, if they induce the reader to approach the work referred to for the first time or anew, I have had all the thanks and satisfaction that I warrant or want.

Utano
29 June 1971

I. Statements & Prefaces

Statement
for *Nonce* (Elizabeth Press, 1965)

To speak of poetry is to apologize for what needs no apology, to explain what needs no explanation—or if the need exists, the poetry has failed and no systematics will improve matters.

These poems, like all poems worth their salt, are meant to be voiced, to be taken into the mouth, breathed from heart and gut, to be resumed by others and the air. Airs for the heirs of air.

A predecessor whom I can only try to re-sound said on a like occasion: "... What I have done is yours; what I have to do is yours ..." Take it and leave it.

28 July 1965

13

Statement
for *Stead* (Elizabeth Press, 1966)

Poetry calls for anonymity. It appeals, in short, to the each in all and the all in each. Its particularity must become yours. Autobiography is implicit in any one's work and may be taken for granted, but what has been realized and so set out as to be shared loses itself in the self that is found extended without end in song.

As the author has elsewhere put it:

If I have nothing to offer you in the face of death—in its stead—the ache behind every ache, the instant man knows, I have no claim as poet. My song must sing into you a little moment, stay in you what presence can muster—of sense more than meaning, of love more than sense, of giving the life given one with the same fulness that brought each forth, each to each from each, nothing left but the life that is going on.

Prefatory Note to
Words for Each Other (1967)

The title of this book is its dedication.

The poems of this book, insofar as they succeed, will need no explanation, will find themselves in you as resourceful breath.

Something in them, in the sounded meanings joined here, should feed something in you that merits sharing—a little life that feels beyond itself the dying implied in every word, in every thing, in every legend man has devised, in ache in ache in ache, invoking the only judgment man is worthy of: love.

Art as Center

We agree: human being wants needs deserves a firm ground for the life of the spirit and the traditional bases have only too obviously gone by the board: whether church or science, astrology or philosophy (which includes Marxism or any other -ism).

Only one possibility remains us, the only one that has endured for us through us: what is now titled ''art''—the coherence realized binding mankind most truly in work as event.

All faiths, though few care to know it, stay, keep meaning alive through us through the works of art that have ''come through.'' Without the Bible no Christianity or Judaism; Christ and Moses would be as vague as Ozymandias. The same holds true of Buddha or Lao-tze, of Socrates or Heracleitus. Art is never an activity of spare time, but rather the activity that spares time—and this is as true of prehistoric man as it is for us today. It may not be necessary to man, but try imagining human being without the *Vedas,* the *Upanishads,* the *Bhagavad-Gita,* the works of Kung and Chuang, the Bible, Homer, Plato, and so forth. Then raze the remaining pyramids at Gizeh, Angkor Wat, the Acropolis, Chartres, Katsura. Destroy the works of Michelangelo, of Rembrandt, of the artists of Ravenna, of Ajanta, of the recently discovered cave-art of Europe and elsewhere. Excise from human memory all music. The love of speech. The love of dance. What is left that is human? And is it the love of dance, love of speech—or rather the speech of love, dance of love?

Wherever man has attended to and responded to the life

provided him—under whatever circumstances (O Lute of Gassir!) —art has occurred: *of necessity.*

Am I merely confusing, as some would have it, art and religion? The terms in themselves tend to a spurious superiority of being, when, in fact, both occur only as the ground of all human being—what other altitude—or not at all, as the human center.

I say "art" rather than "religion," for art is not sectarian, not insistent on any cause of program, needs no church, despite museums. Not that the maker of art need be lacking in devotion to whatever ideal, but this is not the ground of what is shared. (And "shared" is not "divided," no more than love is offered in pieces, if it is offered in the first place.) So I am moved, and moved profoundly, by a Hakuin or a Hopkins, by a Dante and a Homer, by a Chartres Cathedral and a Parthenon, by the Kudara Kannon and park benches by Brancusi. And I feel them beyond any call to study what compelled them as idea: the work tells itself in me, through me, as me, or misses fire.

Art is that more endurable projection of realization given man to feel more fully what he is and what he is of.

This may not be much, but it is all and enough that man is given and is possible: such nature as stays open to all else that shares predicament.

So the man making art is the man making life come alive more truly for others; he knows what all men come to know with more or less acuteness: that each day and each night he is dying. And he is that one who steeped in the dying finding song, enduring sound of sense, can and does put out himself beyond himself for the only meaning: you.

(from *Elizabeth X*, December 1966)

17

Poetry as a Mode of Realization

Somebody sooner or later has to put it down plainly before the issue is lost sight of in the name of apologeticks. Poetry is not striving to become music, or mathematics. At least, in the sense that I am using it here—referring to a use of language such as shares realization: afresh and in a way that sticks like a burr to the human spirit.

It is not "science" and it is not "machinery." The mechanical and scientific may enter into it, as anything else may—but it is a mode of realization, even as music is, or dance, or film, or painting, sculpture, architecture, etc.

We cannot make poetry for the dead, though we must in the nature of what we are take them deeply into account. We feel what is alive in us most. And whatever we make or do—including killing or fashioning funereal monuments—is not for the dead. The dead, fortunately enough, have no further need of us. Nor can we put back the clock or even the earth to some previous condition. We have to manage with what there is, whatever it may be. No one of us is or can be responsible for what obtains, but all have some small share in the scene. And not the least of man's misery derives from those benighted souls who are certain they are more responsible than others and take upon themselves, assume, far-reaching responsibilities, authority, control, power. Those who know better know worse and those who know best, worst. Christ, no doubt, is the image of the son rampant—just as Oedipus was. The new, the young, given the role of authority, of the absolute: the good, the true, the beautiful.

My own practise of poetry may give me some insight into the ways open to poetry, but it can never be ground for any system or prescription. Dr. Williams, bless him, was busy trying to undermine conventional verse practise, realizing, as he did, the irrelevance of most, if not all, of it.

We like to imagine that the problem is one of catching up with the latest gimmicks. In fact, the gimmicks are always ancient. Man has always been as lazy as the situation allowed. When Old Mother Necessity invents, she does more than lay goose's eggs—even golden ones. She produces in the shape of emergency.

Where we are now is at a point in human time—which no clock shall ever compass—that will no longer let us accept the old wisdoms as such, the old faiths. We have traded them in for updated notions: hypotheses, theories, axioms, equations, etc. We trust the logical solutions to logical problems, logically enough. But computers are not going to get hungry, need sexual stimulation, beget children, shit—OR, and we must remember this, get off the pot. Man is a wonder at producing tyranny—the forms change, the fact remains.

The fruit of all this shifting-about is a profound self-questioning, a doubt—and a rooted one—that what we call ''existence''—or if it werent pre-empted by the world of publicity and masscom even as the former is by foolosophy LIFE—has any meaning. The operative word in our TIME is ''meaning.'' This was true already before Wittgenstein made the issue more patent and unblinkable. But it is easy to fall into the trap of assuming this means that SILENCE is MONEY. (It MAY be, but that is only an aspect of human shrewdness, politicks, biznis.) As Beckett, as Wittgenstein himself attests, to be alive and intelligent is to talk—part of the expatiation of ignorance. Even Valéry in all those years of his wellknown silence was busy filling up notebooks with ideas. It may be that what is said will be worthless. It is clear enough that far and away most of what has been said—which dates man—IS precisely worthless. But meaning has always tended to be local, immediate, and effective enough for its purposes—whether to relieve annoyance or share a dream or spread the gospel.

Poetry is a special use of language. Its relation to music—since that is so often pushed—is rather as Zukofsky has sensed it: ''of an order that speaks to all men.'' Memorably, I'd add. What one loves one never forgets. And poetry is always a mutual affair.

19

All sorts of NEW theories have been tossed up for grabs in the past 20 years or so—from Dr. Williams on. Composition by field or a variable foot, free workings, etc. The point I would make is a simple one and it relates precisely to my own experience, which, I feel, is exemplary enough. There is no ONE way. It is clear that any of the traditional approaches must be weighed anew in usage. Each poet nowadays must find the poem occurring; he cannot come truly with some pat answer of how it will look or sound. A poem is an event, but one that is meant to be shared and only insofar as it is shared is it poetry. In short, silence is not poetry, but it is the ground out of which and to which poetry comes and goes—and the silence is ours, that of each one of us *as* each one of us. Poetry is another of the more enduring acts of human community, human communion.

Poetry has an ecological bearing. It is precise to its occasion and wholly given to it. It is of maximum economy, for no other reason than that no human being can or wants to remember what isnt enlivening, what doesnt help sustain livingdying. It is a high protein substance. It is language at its nuclear efficiency. The chemistry of language cannot be reduced to formulas, but there is no doubt of its continuing power of bringing man more into relation with himself and with his situation.

All words touch meaning—beyond mere truth or wisdom. Beyond knowledge. The trite phrase "I love you" remains forceful beyond our petty usages of it—in any language. The phrase is not one that claims truth or wisdom or even knowledge. But it reaches across and MEANS as much as it can, MEANING WHAT IT SAYS IN SAYING IT AS MEANING, AS FEELING.

We have grown accustomed to extracting meaning from event, from poems, from works of art, even as we extract vitamins from foods to feed us them instead of the devitalized foods we create. We trust analysis to reveal a meaning to us and fail to realize that that reductive approach prevents faith and sense of meaning IN EVENT, AS FEELING. We want everything in question and answer form, problem and solution.

The scientist's boast is—Give me a well-stated problem and I'll give you a clear solution. Is that all that is possible? Is it enough? Many problems have been answered long before they were recognized as such. There is a great deal more going on in this world than laboratories admit, or mathematics.

Science, as we know it, as we honor it, is part of a continuing retreat from the total situation into a body whose only function is mentality—each man slowly becoming a little laboratory to experiment on and in. Yes, one day, no doubt, there will be pills, drugs, smokes, that will—under carefully arranged conditions—produce specific types of dreams. Dreams that money can buy. Precisely. Science is part of the continuing drive towards the deterministic vision, towards standardization. It is so convenient. And most of the lives of those yet to be born will be devoted selflessly, no doubt, to the maintenance of conveniences. All men will do as much as they have to in order not to do anything. Until, obviously, the machine—the model hope, the ideal—is perfectly aped, even as it is now envied.

Poetry, as long as it is poetry, must be the vehicle, the transparent medium, whereby the individual finds himself revealed at home in the unknown, with "each other" and with "all."

I myself tend to work out of a most obvious and simple formality of syllables that even a child can grasp—precisely so that it may be "seen through" and used. Not to count syllables, but to see, hear, that the syllables count. That every sound and pause confer meaning upon the moment in the making. This leaves "form" wide open, in the making. The poet's ear, breath, voice, must carry the specifics and in such a way as to invite others to share the breath, the voice, the uniqueness—each in his own way.

The poems, insofar as language can for me, reveal one man's realizations of relation and offer the revelation in such a way that others may share the realizations AS OCCASION. A poem that does not taste to the mouth, that doesnt touch the heart, does not draw the relation of each man to each other and his whereabouts, is for me inadequate.

The poem is yours or no one's.

30 Dec 69

Introduction
to *Back Roads to Far Towns*: Basho's
   Oku-no-hosomichi
Mushinsha/Grossman, 1968

Early one spring morning in 1689 Basho accompanied by his friend and disciple Sora set forth from Edo (old Tokyo) on the long nine-month journey which was to take them through the backlands and highlands north of the capital and then west to the Japan Sea coast and along it until they turned inland again towards Lake Biwa (near Kyoto). Approximately the first half of this journey, the most arduous part, remains recorded in the *Oku-no-hosomichi.*

Basho in his 46th year and Sora in his 41st had lived quietly near each other for some time. The journey was one both had looked forward to and realized would be difficult and even dangerous. And, indeed, one might *not* return. It was to be more a pilgrimage—and in the garb of pilgrims they went—than a case of wandering scholarship: a sight not uncommon even in modern Japan, visiting from temple to temple, seeing old acquaintances, places famed in history or poetry or legend, touchstones for the life lived, the dying to come and what life continues.

By then Basho had already earned a far-flung reputation as a *haikai* poet and master and was much awaited and sought out: he was himself invariably the occasion *for* poetry.

Most of his poetry (and it is within the tradition which he himself was shaping) evokes a context and wants one. The poems are not isolated instances of lyricism, but cries of their occasions, of some one intently passing through a world, often arrested by the momentary nature of things within an unfathomable "order."

If, at times, the poems seem slight, remember that mere

22

profusion, words piled up "about" event, often gives an illusion of importance and scale belied by the modest proportions of human destiny. Precise conjunction of language and feeling, appropriately sounded, directness and fulness in brevity, residual aptness and alertness, mark *haiku* at best (as in those of Basho): grounded in season and particularity, no matter how allusive. "Down-to-earth and firm-grained."

Sora also kept a journal of this trip, but it stays as a strictly factual "check"—while Basho made his into (essentially) a poem (after some years) that has become a center of the Japanese heart/mind.

We too move out with him to and through the backwater regions of north central Honshu. His words are our provision, breath, rhythm. And they can never not be our time. The end of his journey is the end of ours. Everywhere he goes one feels a sounding made, the ground hallowed, hardwon, endeared to him and so to us, through what others had made of it, had reached, discovered.

So many today who have lost touch have lost touch with just such grounds for being.

When tears come to Basho it may seem that he is merely being soppy (one might say the same of Dante or of Stendhal, though both are also "tough"). A man's sentiments, however, are not disputable. But if we feel what it is to live and to be dying, each one alone, know what cherishing is and *see* what Basho sees into tears, we may realize that there is a sympathy that enlarges the spirit without destroying it that obtains for man a more complete sense of relation to his world.

What Basho doesnt say moves at least as much as what he does. One knows his silences go deeper than reasons. And when his eyes plumb words for heart—when the heart holds the island of Sado, locus of exile, at the crest of a brimming sea, and the eye lifts from that pointed violence and loneliness on the horizon to the stars flowing effortlessly up and over and back into the man making vision, who has not at once felt all language vanish into a wholeness and scope of sense that lifts one as if one weighed nothing?

Whether, when we go to him, return to him, as many of us must when we are most alone, we feel much as he does in his last entry, elated, back with old friends, or not, remains for each to find out. But the hope is in bringing his text over into English that

23

some will open wider for it, discover the heart's, spirit's, geography refreshed—"read" (as a Noh teacher said apropos of reading a Noh text) as one who has travelled and climbed and come down and who knows he has still harder going ahead "reads" a map.

Meanwhile a summer's journey awaits, two men are about to depart on foot, one of them already thinks of us.

How far is't now to the end o' the world, my master?
Why, a day's journey . . .

Preface
to *frogs & others*: poems by Kusano Shimpei
Mushinsha/Grossman, 1969

It's difficult to talk and get through to others. To sing is un-
doubtedly better—kinder—happier—and that much rarer and more
difficult. And yet this precisely is what a poet feels called upon—as
one to whom language is faith and resource—to try to do.

In this world committed to PROGRESS it has sometimes
seemed that if ''survival of the fittest'' were to be taken seriously,
we might as well ''stop the music'' and yield the honors to the
amoeba as having long since proven its superiority. Man is
obviously a most latterday upstart—not quite sport—in the scale of
things. And though it seems, and is, hopeless to say so, it is by no
means clear why man should be regarded as any ultimate. No
doubt it can be fairly argued that he is the most complicated of all
things known—but whether that in itself is a cause for congratu-
lation must be left for the gods to determine.

The Orient—thinking principally of India, China and Japan—
has managed somehow through the hardwon intelligence (art) of a
few tough souls to come to a sense of scale—beyond the
equilibrium of sophrosyne—that makes sense, that casts man into
his minimality in the face of the geography of time. This has in no
way eliminated—even under the title of Enlightenment—the
existential ache—though it may provide momentary lapses.

Kusano Shimpei's frogs, familiar as they are at once, are
utterly Oriental configurations. They are the voices of proportion,
muting wisdom even as they suffer it. They are the voices of nature
—in its largest sense—and of absolute innocence. They sing in the

25

face of every moment's doom. They live beyond any idea of PROGRESS. They are the gaiety and spontaneity and love and rootedness of fear in man. They mock our pretensions, but share them too, gently. They are a society whose limits are prehistoric and posthistoric. They live beyond abuse within the nature of man's spirit.

There are more than (or less than, if you will) frogs in Kusano's world, naturally—but the city, the landscapes, the denizens, all find their measure in these small leapers in their inland swamps and pools and rivers. Is it only (!) imagination that makes the Aristophanic croakings their chronicler indites as sweet in their provocation as any of our too often less perceived utterances?

In any event, these poems—painfully of our time—sound perspectives we had long forgotten, or had never remembered, were central to what we are and always must be: human beings.

Preface
to *Things* by Francis Ponge
Mushinsha / Grossman, 1971

> "Let him mature the strength of his
> imagination amongst the things of
> this earth, which it is his business
> to cherish and know. . . ."
>
> *Conrad*

Francis Ponge is one of those poets, and poet he is, through the economy/ecology of his vision, whose work, once known, seems to have been awaiting us for a long time. It seems, suddenly, something that poetry was heading towards. Unknown and familiar.

In his espousal of things, he is less their apologist than their willing spokesman. He elicits from and perceives in the mute world an elaborate and exfoliating expression of relation. How far he goes out through language to embrace things or how far he solicits them through language, through the sounding of himself in language that breaks open into language again, to reach him and us is beyond measuring. But we feel at once held and danced with—by the action of language. The exuberance and confirmation of relation moves us beyond judgment—with clarity. So that the rhetoric sees.

Once you have entered his pine woods you cannot emerge again without a new aura of experience, a deeper savoring, nor can you fail to want to find yourself immediately a pine woods to rediscover too.

Ponge's work is an attempt to extend by exempla the poetic task *par excellence* given us today. He sees it both as an extension of language as an act of relation (words themselves become things—substantive beyond grammatical analysis) and the extension of human intelligence as feelingthought. Here art IS science, con-science. Dazzle and confusion revealing mirror in mirror: the point vanishing in the infinite duress, delight. The mystery of all

27

lucidity. To find one self in sight. Language realized once *more* as environment, community.

Ponge's apparently freely wandering *babillage* is, in fact, of a startling preciseness. He not only hears/sounds/sees the words that occur to him, he renews the pledge of meaning in them, honors it, through his allegiance to them and to the things they are the voicings of. The silence he meets sings. An unashamed shaman music—whose sense is lost in its event—in the integrity of a universe that merely includes us, of which we are a slowly realizing particular.

He is, then, in the true sense of the word, a healer—his pharmacopeia: things as they come clear of/through utterance related, entered, joined, proliferating.

He more than evokes pine woods, carnation, swallow, oyster, pebble, rain—he more than enjoys the moment of ''negative capability'' (that a latterday poet once parsed as ''positive incapacity'' and meant more than the irony he intended)—he illuminates language in the brio of its recognitions, our delectation aroused in it. He communicates, makes us communicants: in a rite that is as new as the sun each day.

September—October 1969

II. Theatre

A Note on *Hamlet*

Given the plight of Hamlet, would suicide have satisfied us? Would his simply having "forgotten" the situation served? If Claudius had succeeded in doing away with his young rival and been himself unexposed in the process, would we have felt content, felt—with a knowing nod of our head—Sad, but—yes—that's the way it is and, since it is, it is good (god's good)?

The worst becomes an adequate best: a best for Job's salvation: faith.

The "tragedy," however, is relived—relieved—only as Hamlet purges himself through commitment beyond thought—though through it—in the death met/entailed. Or how death itself is the lever of what rise, what release, we arrive at. We come clear, so kindled, through this awakening.

The relation to death, to the one death provided each, is the source and thus end of all profound drama. East or West.

Anything less is melodrama or comic evasion, diversion.

Hamlet tries to stand outside, play god, play judge, but finally realizes judgment is played on, laid on, him by his very role-taking. And so he enters the trial directly—his own loss of innocence and his standing beyond innocence clear—bearing the absolute credential of risk—and is released from bondage—beyond need or call of verdict. On the shield, not behind it, now.

4 June 1971

31

The Theatre as Commitment

NOTE: The following comments pick up from the various "serious" essays on contemporary theatre written from 1953-1967 by Eric Bentley in his recent book entitled *The Theatre of Commitment*. These comments are not a critique of his work, nor a review of it. They simply develop ideas from comments made by E. B., with the intention of providing some focus for thought on the subject of a possible theatre today.

1

"The professions of playwrighting and acting which Shakespeare entered as a young man had not existed much more than a generation before him."

The nearest thing to a contemporary theatre that the USA has is the psycho-drama, soloist-style, of a Charles Olson at Berkeley or Ginsberg when he is in high etc. At any rate, they suggest the kind of involvement—total—that is required—and the danger of it.

No playwright of any enduring quality is going to occur in America, unless the theatre itself exists that can accommodate such a playwright—even if only theoretically. As it stands American theatre is every man for himself. Even in universities there is no ensemble. A box-stage can only accommodate a puppet-theatre —which would be O.K. too—but no one in America seems interested in competing with Chikamatsu.

The theatre of "happenings" is simply a recognition that theatre, such as it is, is hopeless and that any way to reach an audience—I half expect assassinations in theatres to become standard fare—is better than none.

But since very few people in the West have ever experienced theatre it is not surprising they have very little sense of it.

When I adduce, as I am about to, some personally known practise in the Noh theatre—by a troupe that is by no means

32

extraordinary (though they do bring the unusual zest of a new family to the ancient art), I'm not saying we must imitate the Noh—no more than pointing at the ancient Greek tragic theatre or Shakespeare I mean that we should do likewise; it is obvious that we cant. But we still can (perhaps) learn something. And the Noh theatre—as exemplary a theatre as one could ever dream of—still manages and still offers unbelievable performances.

The troupe to which I refer, located in Kyoto, one of a number, offers only 4 programs, usually of 3 or 4 plays each, in the course of a year—from the repertory. (It is, of course, a strictly repertory theatre.) There is no director. There is no producer. There are no journalists in attendance, for the performance only occurs once; there is nothing to sell. There are no names in lights. The troupe works together, largely as family, for a lifetime.

After their performances, or even rehearsals, or recitals, there is always at once an open critical session. No punches are pulled, but I have never felt either malice or anger. More often the feeling is one of plain concern, good humor (a lot of repartee flying), keen attention, and gratefulness. Everyone takes a bath, goes out and eats together. There are no profits to add up, since losses are inevitable. The economy is managed through the teaching of part-time amateurs, who also compose a large part of the audience. So that by and large the audience, at this point in Japanese history it is a fair cross-section of the community, young and old alike, mostly working-class, is made up of aficionados.

The audiences are small; it is an intimate theatre. And usually the members of the audience have had some direct contact with the actors in some way. And they almost invariably speak to the performers in the intervals or after the show—not to flatter, but to share the family pride, or whatever feeling is felt.

Until there is a company of performers permanently organized at a theatre or a reasonable facsimile of one with a clear and open policy, whatever it might be, there can be no enduring play-wrighting.

Bentley, in afterthought, in 1967—after his essay of 1953—quotes a squib saying that ''the first permanent federally subsidized professional theatre in the United States, financed by nearly 1 million dollars, was established here (in Los Angeles) today. . . .''

I'd estimate that that theatre will have gone through that subsidy comfortably between the time of that squib and now (early 1969). And it will be soon presenting popular Broadway re-runs, if it continues at all.

Any theatre that has ever occurred has come about through a deeply-rooted interest and satisfaction on the part of the community in which it occurred. Art that endures is more than artificial; it is an enduring need. Not man's only need, to be sure, but a need—like hunger—that craves satisfaction; it is a need to live more keenly and truly the human chance.

2

> "A critic is only a judge. A judge doesnt help you to
> commit your crime or even to abstain from com-
> mitting it. His verdict—too late to influence the
> actions under consideration—has value, if at all, not
> for the prisoner, but for society at large."

A judge who renders a verdict of guilty and a death-penalty to accompany it is of no concern to the prisoner at all? Reading Jerome Frank, who has had plenty of judicial experience, makes one wonder indeed about judges and critics.

Waiting for Godot is not Bentley's cup of tea; he tries to talk it down, while boosting other stock, but the very fact that it keeps bobbing up anyhow, mutes all verdict. The playwright and his work are not under indictment. They are themselves the judges of society. The critic, if anything, is then judging the judges.

But the drama is not fundamentally concerned with judgment, though moral values are inevitably implied in one way or another. As in all art—judgment functions on a preliminary level. In the ultimate offering what remains is realization presented in such a way as to be scored fully by another, in another, through another. This mutes "confession," which rarely allows space for any other and merely begs for private attention, wants cult. Drama is NOT cultic.

Realization—and I see that my use of the phrase "real-theatre" has been picked up already, so that I'd best reiterate before the sense of it is lost—that it refers to the theatre of realization—is NOT merely an intellectual apprehension. It is not simply "understanding" (whatever that might be), but a person so

34

come to his senses as to live anew, more acutely kindly. To present one's realizations in such a way that they CAN be shared fully, and assuming that the realizations are those of a constant depth, requires imaginative genius.

No Rimbaud in his teens can offer us realizations of such depth as we hunger for. He has insights that have yet to find appropriate range and exercise. With his final works we begin to feel the pains of what is more adequately, inadequately, lived. What we are slow to realize, of course, is what he DID realize, in stopping writing poems.

The cult of youth is bathos. I dont mean young people behaving as young people; I mean older people pretending they are still in their twenties or teens. The difficulty of being precisely what one is remains.

Eric Bentley has been America's most serious theatrical critic for several decades now. Has it improved audiences? Has it improved playwrighting? And if he didnt get paid for his articles, would he bother? I wonder, indeed, how often he himself would go to the theatre, if he had to pay his own way.

3

"The theatre today is demoralized." "I should like to oppose to [the] idea of a poet who merely takes the blood pressure of the age the idea of a poet who raises the blood pressure of the age."

The only time the USA (and that, as it happens, covers the whole Western hemisphere) had the semblance of a possible theatre was in the Works Project span—brief enough, but certainly a time of great feeling of possibility. And it wasnt, as far as I recall, the involvement of vast sums of money, but simply that the country at large seemed, as a community, to be bestowing its blessings upon such activity, to be WANTING it and ENCOURAGING it. But it was, like the other signs of theatre in America (Provincetown, Phoenix, etc.) a relatively small proposition. As was and is best. It kept promise intimate, near, approachable. Local. Today, America is convinced that it takes millions to do anything. In fact, it takes very little beyond genuine and clear concern. The community of interest is the only subsidy that truly supports an artist and the artist, naturally, feeds what feeds him.

What demoralizes theatre most today in America is not the failures, but rather the successes, the subsidies, the grants. All the superfluity that calls not for the realizing spirit, but only the alert and himself sold salesman.

Everybody's selling something—which even infects so saintly a soul (I am told) as myself. Or Clayton Eshleman—behold—selling me to you. (I presume you know better—but it is a presumption.)

The poet is not concerned with the blood pressure of an age. He is not a doctor, witch. or otherwise. He is not a teacher; he is an educator, yes, but more he is and feels it exactly—a mortal man. Or woman. He gradually comes to realize that he is ignorant —not out of some twist of humility—and that he is hopelessly so. And this is not peculiar to one age more than another. And it has nothing to do with blood pressure. Or titillation. He knows that whatever meaning may be, may occur, occurs *only between man and man*. And he addresses himself to that plight, as profoundly as he can.

Bentley quotes Mary McCarthy, in a footnote, to the effect that "To the extent that America has any communal life at all, it is centered in the New York theatre; here is the last refuge of sociability and humanism." The lady is—I hope—being ironical; if not, let's just face the fact that community doesnt exist any longer in America—or if it does, it is not obvious to anyone who lives in the urban society of America.

4

"The 'objective' is real, the 'subjective' is unreal—in other words, you get at the truth by getting away from yourself."

Bentley is attacking the ideas quoted above. But he doesnt see that words "real" and "unreal" are the values being pressured. And he still pays homage to the phrase "the truth."

The scientific approach is absolutely prevalent today in educated circles and often well beyond them. It is pervasive. Science is our faith. Buckminster Fuller can in one breath convey

the absolute unpredictability of existence and our complete ignorance and in the next be absolutely certain, buttressed by a great
subsidy, that all human problems can be solved by the computer.
There is no doubt that he is absolutely right. If you can reduce man
to a problem, no doubt a computer will provide solutions. If not for
all, at least for the democratic majority. And isnt that what all the
revolutionaries are fighting for?

We like to diddle with that more tolerant position known,
mischievously in the shadow of Einstein, or is it penumbra, as
relativism. Or we prefer the slightly more sophisticated jargon of
ids egos and superegos. I'm told that the computer is now solving
the "mystery" of Stonehenge. We are slowly realizing how
sophisticated our primitive ancestors were! What will man, or his
mutation, use a million years hence to unravel the mystery of the
computer? Or will the secret be explained in one of our clever
time-capsules or by an unfrozen scientist?

Is theatre real—or unreal? Is it objective—or subjective? Or
are these questions, like ALL questions, pseudo-questions?

5

> "Brecht said, in effect, that you dont paint a still-life
> when the ship is going down. He seems not to have
> realized that you dont paint at all when the ship is
> going down. . . .
> . . . Still-lifes get painted by people who are deter-
> mined to paint them if they are on board ship and
> even if the ship is going down. Sometimes there are
> enough lifeboats. Sometimes land is in sight.''

Bentley is concerned to point out that the artist likes to believe
what he does is of great importance, when, in fact, it matters very
little. Bentley is confusing cases. How important anything is
demands a frame of judgment that is invariably open to debate. The
A-bomb is continually brought up as the great crux of our time,
the nuclear age, etc. And we are all, as happy as children in a
ghost story, dreaming of the great holocaust that will end the
world and only wish, penis-envy, anyone? that we could have the
option of pulling the trigger, pressing the button, or whatever the
little gimmick is that does the trick. In fact, it has made NO

37

difference at all; it has merely seemed to have upped the stakes in the politickal pokergame going on. Let's get down to earth. Not one of us alive will be alive 120 years hence, with or without nuclear weapons. To the dead what does "time" or even "space" mean? (We trust that heaven is extra-spatial—or God would be a greater fool than we have already imagined Him to be.) Your offspring? Let's cut out the crap. The scientists have assured us, give or take a billion years or so that man is doomed. Where are we in all this?

If a man is not fearful of destroying himself—and consider all our young eager drug-takers, whether by prescription or by the more exciting underground route—why should he be chary of anybody else? (Neill of *Summerhill* kindly says that he doesnt mind any child destroying himself as long as he doesnt destroy Summerhill. Well, he doesnt put it quite that way, but that's the drift.)

I mean: we are all sinking ships. Morandi painted stilllifes, small ones at that, all his life and never got as far as Paris, London, or New York, yet will endure as long as man endures as a modern. He makes the trend-setters look like the trend-setters they are. He didnt starve; why? Because he liked to eat, I guess.

6

"There are few persons who cannot be tempted by money. A poet is a person whose temptation to write poetry is so strong that it swamps the temptation to go after money. The poet has a simpler time of it than the dramatist: he makes a vow of poverty and leaves it at that."   (1960)

Even at this late date this quaint romantic notion still exists. And Bentley certainly does try to come on as a hardheaded cookie. It would have helped if he gave us some notable examples—even three, even ONE (1)!

Dylan Thomas? Wallace Stevens? James Dickey? Robert Bly? Auden? Eliot? WCW? Creeley? Levertov? Myself? Not even gentle Ezra. Chances are there have been a few pretenders along the way, but they never came up with poetry.

The vast majority of those we regard as poets today are part-time operators. Unless, like Duncan, say, they have adequate means to make it without resorting to teaching, etc.

One who is poor, who has never had anything, has no vow of poverty to make. And the rich forsake their riches, like Gautama, only when they believe there is another wealth greater than the material wealth they have known.

An extension of this is the sentimentality—and the political sentimentality that runs riot amongst young people and artists today in America and elsewhere is only another sad reflection of the general impotence and self-despair that people who have no use for themselves provide—of a belief in the natural kindness of the poor. The poor share more readily all that they have than the rich. No doubt. When one has nothing, it is easy to share. But the beggar become rich slowly will not share so readily. The truly kind are rare at any level of society. They need make or take no vows; they offer what they can of themselves—hopelessly—as part of the life they share.

7

"A lot of comment on Beckett has gone wrong in taking for granted that Godot will not come, but hope does spring eternal, and even Auschwitz prisoners hoped to get out. In this element of hope lies the politics of the play. Without it, *Godot* would be anti-political, inviting its audience to lose itself in complete despair or to seek redemption from despair outside the world depicted (presumably in the other world of religion)."

Bentley closes his essays with an attempt to enlist Beckett on the side of COMMITMENT. What crude irony!

The name GODOT is enough to tell us that Beckett has no intention of being intimidated, or intimidating us, by having recourse to religion, so-called. And, of course, the play is anti-political. How could Beckett accept politicks as anything but painfully comic arrogance?

And of course, the play is undermining our customary ploys in the business of plying hope. Hope, for Beckett, as it must, stinks. Is a lie. A white lie? Maybe. But he realizes how easily it swells and becomes politicks. As Bentley does not. As few do.

The issue is not whether Godot is coming or not. There is no issue. There is only, as Eliot might say, the waiting. And it is a waiting without any real (?) expectation. It is waiting without hope and nevertheless waiting, unable to abandon the ghost "unnaturally" and so conceding time and making a vaudeville out of it to "pass the time." There is only the simple physical attachment to being, which requires another to assume the dimension of even seeming.

Is it theatre? Does it matter?

It is realization, it is real-theatre. And if it isnt enough, nor *Endgame,* and they ARENT enough, we have only one option: to offer profounder realizations. Poetry is always about to be born. Beware: you may HAVE to live.

Utano
18 February 1969
(from *Caterpillar* No. 7, April 1969)

The Noh

". . . the sudden illumination—
We had the experience but missed the meaning,
And approach to the meaning restores the experience
In a different form, beyond any meaning
We can assign to happiness. . . ."

T. S. Eliot: *The Dry Salvages*

Many comparisons have been made between Noh and various forms of Western theatre. None of them has any validity and none is useful.

Best to come to the Noh, for the first time, without the confusions of what it MIGHT be. What it is awaits you and, if you move with it motionlessly, listen and see, it will stay with you as an always final scene.

Somewhere I have written, with Noh in mind:

Nothing happens in these plays: everything, in a sense, has already happened: now on stage comes the realization.

The "facts" of Noh history are clear enough. (We have some direct texts from Ze-ami on the subject.) As P. G. O'Neill in his *Early Noh Drama* states it: "During the 14th and 15th centuries Noh plays formed part of several types of entertainment, of which the most important were Sarugaku and Dengaku. The basis of Noh drama as it is known today was established by two Sarugaku players, Kanze Kan-ami Kiyotsugu (1333-1384) and his son Ze-ami Motokiyo (1363-1443), and their most important innovation was the absorption into Sarugaku of the music and songs of Kusemai, one of the many minor entertainment forms of the period."

Certainly Kan-ami drew on all the resources available in his day—dance, poetry, legends, costume, music, temple spaces, etc.

41

Often he seems, and Ze-ami both with and after him, to have remodelled with remarkable vigor and insight existing materials. In this, not unlike dear Shakespeare or, indeed, even the ancient Greeks.

Father and son (and other members of the proliferating family gradually) put the show on the road and, for all the vicissitudes the Noh has known through the centuries and its decline from any central popularity, it retains—even in its many metamorphoses—the thrust and heart/mind (*kokoro*) that its makers intended.

The very survival in force of the Noh tradition for some 600 years testifies to its power. There are those who find it out of joint with our times—harking back as it does to ancient beliefs largely put by now—but the release into openness that its dance invariably effects remains—when truly performed—as vital to man as it ever was and will be.

The Noh is extraordinary for the slow clarity of its economy, its ability to penetrate event and human nature with minimal action—letting the words sing and tell, the actor break free with a profound and inimitable exactitude. (Every step and beat, every drummer's cry, is foreknown and yet surprising when it occurs as it must.)

By and large the Noh is a poetic experience; that is, the text LEADS and SCORES the performance. Since a loss of text does deprive the viewer, especially the Western viewer, of nuance (for what mime occurs is kept carefully reduced to essence), we have tried to provide below at least the continuity of the piece you are about to witness and to translate out (as well as offer a romanized reading of the Japanese words) some of the textual highlights.

. . . . . .

Motomezuka (moh-toh-meh-zoo-kah) is reliably reputed to be by Kan-ami (at least in its basic lines); there are numerous textual variations used by different schools. The title means: *The Sought-For Tomb.* It is one of the oldest known pieces in the canon (which contains about 250 plays—the vast majority of which were composed by the end of the 15th century).

Mikata Ken has written of this play that it is of "strong build." The costume of the *nochi-sh'te* (the key actor in the final half)—he notes—is not designed for dancing "but for doing"—

relating the play to other pieces of self-discovery and release of the soul from the hell of life, pieces like *Higaki, Kinuta* and *Sotoba-Komachi*. And it holds, he asserts, an important position as one of the original plays in the canon.

(A complete translation, for those interested, may be found in Volume II of the Nippon Gakujutsu Shinkokai's *Japanese Noh Drama* [reprinted by Tuttle]. It is not an inspired rendering and tends to over-poeticize clear words, but it is reasonably accurate along its lines and is well annotated.)

Kondo Kenzo—who plays the lead role (the *sh'te*)—is the current head of the Hosho school (based in Tokyo) and is generally and rightfully regarded as one of the finest living Noh performers. His "style" might be called "unadorned" or "naked." There is no striving for effect. I once remarked of his acting: "He does nothing 'right' and he can do nothing wrong." When a man's life in its fulness is brought to bear in such theatre, the open performance becomes its own judgment and mutes ours. We can only be wondrously grateful at the chance to be present. (The man is in his 80s now.)

The Hosho school is particularly noted for its unpretty singing style: it often sounds guttural, deepthroated, syllable-swallowing. As if it refused any decoration or advantage of the merely poetical. The singing is all breath in articulation and meaning occurs within event.

Motomezuka is (of the 5 groups or kinds of Noh plays) of the 4th category: a *shunen-mono*: a story of a suffering spirit that has not as yet found release from hell. This play is fairly typical of its kind. It moves—after a quiet lyrical first half—to an intensely religious finale. The "dance" is inner-contained (warranting the use of a mature actor) rather than the more gratuitous dance of joy or appeasement that often concludes a Noh play.

The "plot" has been drawn from a "long" poem in the *Manyoshu* (the most ancient and most famous of the Japanese anthologies): Volume IX, No. 1809—which relates how two young men were attracted by the same girl. She (Unai-Otome) distressed at finding herself the cause of their grief drowned herself. And they, in turn, at her burial mound killed themselves in ardent despair. A later extension of the story in the *Yamato Monogatari* (*Yamato Stories*) adds more color and Kan-ami would seem to have drawn principally from this source.

Numerous lines are enlisted from a variety of other old poems—particularly in the first half of the play. In the latter part—the poetry draws upon the *Lotus Sutra*. The early spring/late winter feeling that pervades the first half is more than thawed-out in the hellfire imagery of the pent-up spirit in the latter half.

Japanese critics have all remarked the unusually strong—and perhaps excessive—images of torment the girl undergoes.

. . . . . .

The stage is empty. Ancient pine painted on the back wall. The sacred place. From beyond the first sounds of music, the musicians practising, reveal that the play is about to begin.

After the musicians (flute and then 3 drums) have entered quietly—and all move with feet never leaving the ground—as the voice is rooted in the gut—and taken their places along the backstage, the chorus, or the front line of it, enters via the rear sliding door just beyond the porch at the right (painted over by bamboo), and seat themselves on the porch, fans closed set before them on the sacred (*hinoki*: Japanese cypress) wooden floor. Then, from the bridge, come two stage attendants bearing a frame ''mound'' ˉ draped over by a deep-colored cloth and place it carefully in front of the drummers at backstage center.

Once they are satisfied and have removed themselves—probably to the back wall left—the entrance music commences. Flute and drums, at changing intervals, lead in along the bridge (the 5-striped curtain at the back end of it lifted by two bamboo poles at either lower end up and in) the *waki* enters (in this play, as often, a *bonze,* in pointed hood, plain kimono and broad-sleeved over-robe that reaches almost to the knees, closed fan, hands always at hips). He is followed, at discreet interval, by another monk (*tsure*) in similar vestments.

The *waki* and his *tsure* (one or two, as the case may be) enter the stage on their journey and take positions facing each other on either side in front of the prop. They sing their travelling song opening: ''Long is the journey through the land/making towards Miyako.'' The chorus (*ji*) repeats the words in whisper-form. The *waki* then identifies himself as a bonze from the other side of Honshu on his first trip to the Capital (Miyako), Kyoto. He and the others continue together moving towards their posts at the

44

right side of the stage and sing their song of travel: how for some days they have been journeying by land and water until they now reach the famed fields of Ikuta (= Life Field)—part of presentday Kobe—a place known for its herbs in the ancient poetry. They decide—as the *waki* says—to wait for some natives to turn up and then to enquire of them about the place in greater detail. They seat themselves. The stage is open again.

Entrance music (*issei*).

The *sh'te* (a village girl) in young woman mask, black wig, gold brocade and broadsleeved robe, fan in right hand, herb-basket in left, finally appears beyond the curtain and moves to the third pine; the other girls (*tsure*) with her, in similar costume, stop further along the bridge. They face each other and sing. They sing of the rigor of gathering herbs in early spring/late winter: dividing and sharing the words between them. As the words all fall together they sing:

Sh'te:	mi-yama ni-wa
	matsu-no yuki dani
	kiena-kuni
Tsure:	Miyako-wa
	nobe-no wakana tsumu
	koronimo
	ima-wa narinuran
	omoiyaru koso
	yukashikere
Sh'te:	koko-wa mata
	motoyori amasakaru
	hinabito nareba
	onozakura
	uki-mo inochi-mo
	Ikuta-no umi-no
	mino kagirinite
	uki waza-no
	haru-to shimonaki
	ono-ni dete
Together:	wakana-tsumu
	iku satobito-no
	ato naran
	yukima amatani
	no-wa narinu

45

michi nashi totemo
fumiwakete
michi nashi totemo
fumiwakete
nozawa-no wakana
kyo tsuman
yukima wo matsu naraba
wakana-no moshiya
oimosen
arashi fuku
mori-no kokage
one-no yuki-mo
nao saete
haru toshimo
nana kusa-no
Ikuta-no wakana
tsumoyo
Ikuta-no wakana
   tsumoyo

---

deep
     mountain
snow on pines
not gone yet
        but
in Miyako's
       fields
early herb gathering
time—as is likely—
    has come round
ah
   the thought of it
        sweet
here
    far from there
country folk
       ay
lead a hard life
eking existence out
engaged in labor

out in O-no
                    (Smallfield)
not yet spring

gathering young herbs
many country footprints these
must be
            traces
                        snow free
revealing ground

even pathless
pushing through
   even pathless
       pushing
through.

The three girls enter stage as they complete their song:

from field and marsh
let us gather
                        young herbs
today
to wait till the snow
has utterly gone
the greens will have turned
            too old
storm sweeping
            the wilderness
cold still
            snow at O-no
seven the herbs
            of spring now
Ikuta's young greens
let us cull O
Ikuta's young greens
    let us cull
                        O.

The *sh'te* at center and the *tsure* find themselves now
addressed by the *waki*—who has risen.
The first exchanges reiterate the scene and the girls explain
what they are doing. Finally the bonze asks where the famed

47

Motomezuka (the legendary tomb of Unai-Otome) is. The girls claim no knowledge of it—the *sh'te* insistent upon this point—and now say they must be off about their work. They lightly rebuke the *waki* for wasting his time there and wasting theirs with idle questions. They must go—as they say—to find lean pickings in the snowbound fields. They would be content with "young sprouts with old leaves." The chorus—which has begun to sing—deepens the mood throughout and adds a feeling of extra-dimension. Allusions to ancient love stories occur in imagery of herb-gathering. In the end—via the chorus—they abandon their task because of the severity of the season.

The *tsure* rise and leave (by the back exit); only the *sh'te* remains. Not surprisingly the bonze asks her why she alone has stayed. She—it would seem—had been touched by his asking for the Motomezuka and offers to lead him there—which she then does. Then turns and seating herself near the tomb relates the tale of it to the listening priests.

Once upon a time—she says—there lived in Ikuta a maiden by the name of Unai-Otome. Two young men from different nearby villages had evidently become aware of her charms and, enamored of her, declared on the very same day through letters their devotion. Unable to decide their claims, she preferred not to choose rather than stir up resentment between them. They—unsatisfied—challenged each other, then, to an archery contest—to see who could first kill a certain mandarin-duck (the symbol from time immemorial of conjugal bliss and fidelity) on the Ikuta River. The upshot was that they both struck the target simultaneously. The girl hearing of the event and feeling responsible for the death of the revered bird drowns herself (shades of Ophelia) ironically in the very same river (the River of Life) and is buried in the tomb, now visible, behind her. But the young men, so spurned by the girl's act and in their guilt, kill themselves. And this act—in Buddhist fashion—binds the girl to the wheel of life yet—as a sinner—and she realizes it WITHIN her death (as the chorus tells ending the first part) and desires only absolution. She rises—even as they sing the action—and slowly vanishes into the tomb. And slowly vanishes into the tomb.

During the interval (when the audience feels inclined to cough and move about) the music is silent and the *sh'te*—within the prop—is transformed by an attendant behind the tomb. A *kyogen* actor—who has—perhaps unnoticed—been seated at the back of the bridge at the first pine—rises and comes on stage to center. He is a local inhabitant (always on yellow socks) and is asked by the *waki* to tell in full the Motomezuka legend. This he does, for about 15 minutes, in polite but demotic language—which the audience can readily follow without book—if they wish. (There are—uncommon—occasions in the Noh canon when the interlude does in fact have comic impetus. Such plays or sections reflect later work by and large. And are sometimes optional variations—as in *Yashima.*)

The *kyogen* performer sits at stage center, after a brief dialogue with the bonze, and delivers the lengthy monologue in a sequence of long phrases—in a loud voice and in a style that we may find rather similar to the dry recitative of opera relative to the more singing passages of the play proper.

The texts used for the interludes are NOT provided in the song books (which many in the audience, you will notice, use for following the words and more especially the particular modulations of a given performance: the books being "scored"). The words are the preserves of the *kyogen* schools. (They can be obtained, of course, by interested persons.)

. . . . . .

The *kyogen* finishes and takes leave of the *waki*. He usually returns first to his bridge station before unobtrusively exiting by the rear sliding door during the *waki*'s first speech in the concluding section.

The *waki* bonze and his sidekicks pick up the opening of the finale; the agony and release. They sing a prayer from sacred text (sutra) in behalf of the lost soul of Unai-Otome that she may gain enlightenment, release and thus attain Buddhahood.

The tomb now draws attention as the *sh'te*'s "grave" voice (that of the hell-dwelling spirit of the lost maiden) issues from within:

Nochi-sh'te: O
(Unai-Otome)   koya hito marenari
                waga kofun narade
                mata nanimonozo

                    kabane-wo arasou
                         moju-wa
                    satte mata nokoru
                    tsuka-wo mamoru
                         hibaku-wa
                    shofu-ni tobi
                         denko choro
                    naomotte
                         manako-ni ari
                    kofun okuwa
                    shonen-no hito
                    Ikuta-no na nimo
                         ninu inochi

Chorus: (ji)
         satte hisashiki
         kokyo-no hito-no
Nochi-sh'te: Minori-no koe-wa
                    arigataya
Chorus: (ji)
         ara
              enbu koishi-ya!

Unai-Otome: O
              in this vast field
              no life to be seen
              only my old grave

              Rooted monsters
              ugliness
              hanging on
              souls aflame
                 clinging to the tomb
              blown by the wind
                 among pines
              lightning flash
                      morning dew
              hold my eyes
                 So many graves
              those of the young—
              belying
                 the name
                         Ikuta

50

Chorus: After so
      long absence
      comes to my village
        someone
Unai-Otome: lifting voice
        in prayer—
      to my everlasting
          thanks
Chorus: Oh!
      How I yearn
        for the world!

The chorus—as you will note—speaks—as almost always—FOR the *sh'te*—usually the deepest feeling and the aggregate voicing can be immediately sensed as weight. (*Sh'te* and *chorus* never sing together.) Noh singing—drawn from *hara* (gut)—is more open in its voicing than conversation and is decidedly masculine in range. Rather like calligraphy, the attack must be sharp and clean and the end of the breathline likewise (even when breath has been exhausted). The subtlety of the singing is hard to realize without considerable familiarity, but the rhythmic movement and the rich inner effects can be recognized even at first hearing. (Many members of the Japanese audience study the music and have—thus —a direct interest and keen appreciation of what they hear.)

    The LEADER of the chorus (usually seated one in on the back row) gives the cue of pace and emphases to the others and he—like the musicians—bases his ''projection'' on the *sh'te*'s performance. (Noh has very little full ensemble rehearsing—but the Hosho is an extremely tight-knit group and perform well as a unit.)

    The chorus carries on from the above text—singing of the agonies—infinite in the infinitesimal—of human reflection and the inability of the lost soul to find release from the ''Burning House'' (human existence). As the song ends, the backstage attendants come on from behind the prop and remove the mound covering.

    We see the maiden-spirit of Unai-Otome (in a lean woman mask, wig, gold-brocade, white twill over-garment and a [usually] lightblue broad divided skirt) seated on a black-drum-stool within.

    Dialogue now ensues between *waki* and *nochi'sh'te* (the lead actor in the finale) until she rises and dramatically emerges.

    The *bonze* urges the suffering spirit to purge her heart/mind of past delusions and so break free of all human aches and enter the realm of blessedness.

51

The spirit begins to feel that finally she has a chance of release from her fiery hell. She feels again the entreaties of her former ill-fated wouldbe lovers—each pleading for her for himself. She wonders where to turn. A terrible monster like an iron mandarin-duck pecks at her head (a scene not unlike that of *Prometheus Bound* in its savagery). She begs the *waki* to intercede for her. The bonze has—it seems from his words—been brought to share her hell torment and images of conflagration rage on all sides. Impossible to escape. The *sh'te* coming alive more and more agonizingly. (The *waki* always ROCK to the *sh'te*'s fluidity.)

The tomb-prop becomes the Burning House. Escape is frustrated. And then—trying to embrace the burning pillar—chorus singing—the spirit rises again and slowly, as the chorus picks up from her, dances forth:

Nochi-sh'te: Shikojita
          okiagareba
Ji: Shikojita
    okiagareba
    goku-sotsu-wa
    shimoto-wo atete
    otsutatsureba
    tadayoi idete
    hachi-dai jigoku-no
    kazukazu
        kurushimi-wo tsukushi
    onmaenite
        zange-no arisama
            misemosan
    mazu
        tokatsu-kokusho-shugo
    kyokan-daikyokan
    ennetsu-gokunetsu-muken-no soko-ni
    sokusho zuge to
        otsuru aidawa
    mi-tose mi-tsuki-no
        kurushimi hatete
    sukoshi kugen-no
        hima kato omoeba
    oni-mo sari
        kaen-mo kiete
    kurayami to

narinureba
ima-wa kataku-ni
kaeran to
aritsuru sumika-wa
izukuzo to
kurasa-wa kurashi
anato-wo tazune
konata-wo motomezuka
izukuyaran
motome motome
tadori yukeba
motome etari-ya
motomezuka
kusa-no kage-no no
tsuyu kie gieto
moja-no katachi-wa
usenikeri
moja-no kage-wa
usenikeri.

Unai-Otome: Finally
rising
Chorus:
Finally rising
hell-demons whip me out
toss me staggering
stumbling out
through all the tortures
of the eight great
hells suffering
and in repentance
now tell you
first
of the alternation
of life and death's
hell,
of whitehot
iron cable,
of iron mountains
spiked with swords,
of anguished

53

                cry and cry
hell's heat and fury
        scorching
and last
        the hell of eternal
                torture
down down
        to the pit of
                these hells
tumbling
        head over heel
                plunging
three years
        and three months
                suffering
and now feel
        some respite
the demons
        faded
the fire
                vanished and
dark so dark
        has it grown
now must I think to
        return to
                the Burning House
where is my house
groping in
        utter darkness
here seeking
                the grave
wandering
        groping
          searching searching
                where is it
having searched ah
        the soughtfor grave
                is found

Like dew on the grass
        of the shadowy field
                gone
like dew on the grass

of the shadowy field
                    gone gone O
     the spirit's form
              has passed away
     the spirit's shadow
              has passed away.

With these last words the *sh'te* returns to the grave, finds quiet seat at last as the play (words and music and action) ends.

    .   .   .   .   .

There is no *need* to applaud and the silence reverberates without it: but it has become the fashion and is likely to occur at all performances, except those where there is open request otherwise.

The *sh'te* rises and quietly and slowly takes his exit down the bridge and under the curtain that lifts at his arrival. *Waki, tsure* and musicians—at discreet intervals—follow unhurriedly through the curtain way. The chorus exits at the rear.

The stage is again empty. And full. The ancient pine painted there retains its mastery.

                          *

Program Notes prepared for
the Kyoto Kanze Kaikan
14 May 1970

In Japanese each syllable receives equal stress normally and the sounds are consistent.

Sh'te: shteh
Waki: wah-key
Tsure: tsoo-ray
Ji: gee (as in gee-whiz)
Ki-roku-da: key-rockoo-dah
Taro: tah-row
Ze-ami: Zay-ah-me

III. Oral Poetry

Notes Toward an Oral Poetry

I: The voice as the Poetic Immediator

"Sound is fire," and though that isnt Heracleitus but *Against Wisdom As Such,** I'm willing to dig here. Phonetics aims at a kind of precision in the ejaculation of speech and it deals with the care of pronunciation by describing the physiology of the throat and the mouth in its various parts touched by tongue or teeth as air passes through. I am less concerned with a correct pronunciation or the descriptive legalities of phonetics than with the values of whatever sounds the voice projects, or shapes forth. The chief of these, for poetry, of course, is language, the possibility of speech, words.

Since the days of papyri, parchment, and Gutenberg, Aldus, Froben, & Co., oral transmission has fallen into writing and upon the printed page. And poetry has changed notably in the process. Collingwood remarks in his *Idea of History* that there is progress in history, but that in art there is only development. In any event, certain progresses like the book, if we want to consider such a "progress," contain the seeds of an artistic development. And the course that poetry has taken for many centuries now, wherever literature has been printed in quantity, was determined in large measure by the page, the visual document. And the voice receded. There are, of course, comparative exceptions like Shakespeare, say, when the "writing" was set up for a very live stage and

---

*Charles Olson, *Black Mountain Review,* Spring 1954 (reprinted in *Human Universe*).

oftentimes found its revisions, if not actual make upon the boards. Or Donne, whose poems reflect, often, the voice of the preacher coming forth. Or Garcia Lorca, in our own time, whose poetry was known first "by heart" and by ear (voice) before it reached the printed page.

However, what I am driving at is not an elimination of anything. The written poem has become a specific mode, possibility of poetics. What concerns me here is a specific new possibility offered by means as revolutionary, in a sense, as the printing press was in its day. I refer to the recording machine: and, in particular, to the tape-recorder. As a device, strictly-speaking, this machine is capable of perfect transcription of the human voice, where the only distortions need be those intended. The recording can be played over and over again innumerable times and reproduced onto discs or onto other tapes.

When I consider this "progress" in the human potential of communications I am not theorizing. For several months now I have been making poems *directly* onto such a machine. What was pure experiment when I started, curiosity, has become an extended and exciting awareness that this event is not my own possession, but belongs to those who are capable of doing something with it. And I want here, and in successive articles, to set down with more or less detail the range of its possibilities and its nature.

There is no gainsaying certain properties of the printed page: the chance to SEE what it is that the author has put down, whether to see its shape on the page or to study the language, in its various parts, the syntax, the moving accents, etc., etc. But fixed as words are on the page, they are extremely arbitrary in their substantiation. Perhaps this is unclear. My contrast is with such oral poetry as I have in mind. When one makes a poem immediately via his voice, the voice is an exact immediacy. No interpretation interferes in the listener's apprehension of what is happening. (Quite apart from how completely the listener understands what is heard, there is the involvement of direct participation, without any modifying element. The listener doesnt hear his own voice, but that of another, speaking to him in intimate terms, or with such direction as to be completely contingent.) Words on the printed page are at once an approximation of the poet's exact intent, or even the poem's intent. Just as the notes of a string quartet on the sheet of music are not the precise counterparts of the composer's intent, but a rough copy, and undergo inevitable interpretation. It is a parallel development and equally remarkable that a new music is being created today via electronic machines whose range is practically as great and precise as the human ear or mind can compass.*

In short, the word spoken and given the cogency of poetry, its concentration and all the nuances of inflection (which are always immediacies, snatched from the air, as it were, and hot) has a power in communication that the written word cannot hope for. In addition, this new possibility brings poetry back into the full stream of current human life. It becomes at once available to all. So much of its mystery becomes again a mystery that can be felt and understood, because the voice is such a known element. Its fire is clear and real. The ear can sense itself being touched and the air made warm.

There are no doubt dangers of imposture and impropriety and so forth. Dangers there always are in any such event. They must be realized and faced. But the voice is itself a true thing and it requires, when it is true, only listeners for its peculiar persuasions. And it becomes again one man talking to another at the truest level. Where the tone tells the trueness of the rhetoric and the syntax is the way a man's breath holds or races or breaks.

Pierre Emmanuel has told me that he couldnt create such a poetry, since his own is one of carefully modulated revisions. So it is. And yet revisions are not needed here: the very errors speak their vision. René Char says he cannot create such a poetry, yet his own work struggles toward the very subtleties of speech that the ache of the breath as it expresses its love for a river or a day or a country communicates. And the breath itself is such an amazing matrix, telling indelibly its limitations, its life, its implicit death.

It is that marvellous an essence, the breath as the voice makes it, moved by the mind. So that speech is imagination and imagination breathes. And the air takes fire, gives light.

(from *Origin* 1st Series, No. 15, Winter-Spring 1955)

---

*Karlheinz Stockhausen, "Une Expérience Electronique," *La Musique et Ses Problèmes Contemporains,* Juillard, 1954.

Notes Toward an Oral Poetry

> *"I am myself a part of what is real, and it is*
> *my own speech and the strength of it, this*
> *only, that I hear or ever shall."*
>
> Wallace Stevens

II: The Make of the Voice

Again and again I have heard people say that they cant say in a letter what they want to say, that they need to speak to the "other" in person, directly. I have heard people in speaking, for example, of Dylan Thomas's remark that his reading of his poems (or anyone's) made them better than they were on the page.

Now, although it can be cogently argued that fine writing can make itself "heard" on the page and it always does (that is one of its most "telling" effects), it is impossible to imagine that fine speech hasnt certain possibilities denied to the written word. Perhaps it is more accurate to say simply that the oral word, or to get down to my business: the oral poem, is a different possibility from the written counterpart.

The most significant differences are, I think, these. The oral poem is created out of a single condition, a run of time that is exactly co-continuous with its expression. The voice has the contingency of this "condition" or "pressure"; it is a continually sensed "limit." (I put so many words in quotes to indicate their spread of meaning and their tentativeness.) The voice, as such, clues the mind in the progress of the poem in ways that are distinctively oral: i.e., by intervals between words, say, when thought is protracted or when, between syllables often, the sense of a tone or a sound is fully savored, or by pitches of intensity that are so subtly graded that no notation could record them. The voice, via its natural breath-emotional habits, creates the rhythms that participate with the mind in the make of a poem. For the time

62

being I am not going to discuss the values all this creates for the listener, though this aspect is not discontinuous with the experience involved ever. Nor will I discuss in this section the ways written poetry tries to accommodate such possibilities and transforms them into others.

Before I go on, however, I would like to emphasize beyond forgetting what more recent students of prosody (who are open-minded)* are discovering as an essential fact in the make of poetry, that speech and the word as a substance of sound-meaning in the press of the mind create, in utterance, poetic form. (I'm not trying to define what poetry is. It is evident from contemporary practise that it is much broader in its capacities than many centuries have allowed.) This statement sounds perhaps too urgently scientific in tone, when what I am driving at is that the voice trained by condition and the mind, in effecting the most concentrated orders and ardors of language, makes poems. That prose partakes of the same fire seems hardly to need saying, yet it is a rather modern realization:

August 21st, 1877, Hopkins writes to Bridges:

". . . Why do I employ sprung rhythm at all? because it is the nearest to the rhythm of prose, that is the native and natural rhythm of speech, the least forced, the most rhetorical and emphatic of all possible rhythms, combining, as it seems to me, opposite and, one would have thought, incompatible excellences, markedness of rhythm—that is rhythm's self—and naturalness of expression. . . . My verse is less to be read than heard. . . ."

Certainly he did introduce rhythms that had never been so fully sensed and exploited before, even to the point of absurdity sometimes or sound-blindness. Part of this effort, I believe, as with Whitman, who broke structure more informally from its dead or dying conventions, or with Baudelaire or Rimbaud (to jump the language-barrier), was due to a greater personal intensity and

---

*D. W. Harding, "The Poetry of Wyatt," *The Age of Chaucer*, Penguin Books.

illumination being brought to bear. (It is irrelevant for me here to go into a discussion of what this implies of a societal or cultural break-up.) There were things to be said that needed to be drawn free of established matrices and it was only "natural" that speech would lead the way.

After all, if a man can "say" in speech, in conversation, what moves him and make what he says itself moving, why shouldnt he have some way of putting it down for others or making it available? It is what I have been calling for some time the artist's "responsibility," his "ability to respond" becomes his compulsion or propulsion to create a response that can move of itself; this is his responsibility. The response that creates response.

Shakespeare's poetry assumes the theatrical language of the day, a language of high sound and spectacle, of marked drama. Donne's which is not wholly unlike Shakespeare's in many ways, becomes a somewhat more personal voice, where the drama falls from the pulpit. By Milton the voice has become heavily weighted with rhetoric to conduce to a tractarian dignity, a learned writing that achieves its finest strokes when the agony, say, of his blindness tears through. With Wordsworth there is the conscious simplification of rhetoric toward speech, but often bound by the conventions of the written page. With Hopkins, as well as many others increasingly, the voice begins to assert itself, less in its dramatic aspects as in its lyrical aspects and the lyric begins to shape itself to larger uses. No longer simply a poem to be set to music and necessarily curt, but a lyrical structure capable of any number of switches: as in Eliot or Pound or Williams, in English.

Over and over again, the voice in its condition makes our paths for us. Poetry takes form out of the living substance of speech, the breath shapes.

Paris, May 11th, 1955

(from *Origin,* 1st Series, No. 16, Spring-Summer 1955)

The Structure of Poetic Rhythms
in relation to an oral poetry

1. *Opinions:*

".... our poetry has a more intimate connexion with the conversational style of enunciation. . . .

"[in regard to Greek and Latin] *read the verses according to the spoken accent and the full metrical quantity both;* and from these authentic elements let the practical ear work out a rhythm to please itself. . . ."

> John Stuart Blackie
> *On the Rhythmical Declamation of the Ancients,* 1852

".... Rhyme and metre always give one's words a character of necessity—of discipline imposed upon them from outside, while my own verse is never anything save a 'cry from the heart'. . . .

".... What a fluid medium writers like ourselves work in! No wonder that the rules of prosody are invoked to give it, at least from the outside, an appearance of artificial rigidity. . . ."

> Paul Claudel
> *Letters to Jacques Rivière,* 1927
> (English translation)

".... We speak and hear syllables of almost every possible variation of quantity between the obvious longs and the obvious shorts. Such variable material cannot provide a basis for recognizable structure. . . .

". . . If argument, message and emotion lose their order, beauty and shape in the process of communication, they lose their poetic significance. . . ."

Catherine Ing
Elizabethan Lyrics, 1951

". . . that verse will only do in which a poet manages to register both the acquisitions of his ear *and* the pressures of his breath. . . .

". . . What we have suffered from, is manuscript, press, the removal of verse from its producer and its reproducer, the voice, a removal by one, by two removes from its place of origin *and* its destination. . . ."

Charles Olson
Projective Verse, 1950

". . . granted that the best of what the best of us write comes to us by way of the ear, is there a valid reason why it should not be studied and understood? . . .

". . . the foot, since we have to use some sort of technical term to be understood, not necessarily to let it govern our actions, the foot must be understood in a modern world as variable. . . ."

William Carlos Williams
On Measure, 1953

". . . The Sound-aspect of a tongue is its most concrete aspect; and one learns from it . . . to feel language as an *energeia*, not an *ergon*. . . .

"Pronunciation is always in advance of notation."

Nicholas Bachtin
Introduction to the Study of Modern Greek

". . . Most of the words (monosyllables) have more than one unstressed form, depending partly on the style of speech, partly on the preceding and following sounds, and partly on the rhythmic succession of syllables in the context."

Introduction to *Webster's Collegiate Dictionary*, 1943

"*. . . one stress makes one foot,* no matter how many or few syllables. . . ."

Gerard Manley Hopkins
Letter to R. W. Dixon, Feb. 27, 1879

2. *The Oral Structure of Poetic Measure*

Certain essential problems must be considered at this point in comparing the oral poem and the written poem. By the "oral poem" I mean the poem created by the voice directly onto a recording (without rehearsal and *not* mere recitation). The oral poem, a peculiarly contemporary event, can establish more precisely for us the nature of what the essential structure of a poem is, since it itself is a unique and authoritative event; it is precisely its event.

First, however, I would like to open up the problems of poetic structure that need study and considerable definition now before discussing in detail the structure of the oral poem, but using my experience of the oral poem to illuminate these problems.

As I see them, the problems are these:

1. To examine poetic structure in relation to its oral expression;
2. To discover, if possible, the essential nature of poetic rhythms in terms of their structure;
3. To arrive at a practicable theory of poetic measure, one that can cope with contemporary practise and perhaps to establish a firmer base for any future consideration of the structure of poetic rhythms, of poetic form.

It is beyond my present concern, I may as well say at once, to explore the inner machinations of the mind as it predisposes itself toward specific expression. Every poem has its prehistory, but let me take it for granted so as to get immediately onto the ground of the poem itself and strike into the practise. Poetic theory can never depart from poetic practise without becoming mere academicism.

What I have found is that:

The breath is the unit of poetic energy.

The voice, as the articulator of expression, is the shaper of poetic style or personality, but always in conjunction with the ear. I.e., the voice and the ear (which supposes inevitably the mental faculty) modulate the breath.

The relation of the heartbeat to the breath will control the rhythmic impulse.

The breath leads to the structural unit, which is the single struck syllable and its accessory expiration (whether sounded or mute). Both together, for convenience sake, we call the "foot." A single drawn breath and its expiration, however, can accommodate two or three feet (possibly more in rare cases). I would call this breath-unit the "breath-phrase," the "phrase" or the "colon"* (which has begun to be an accepted term in the analysis of Greek metrics).

Within a given colon there can be, under control, several accentual possibilities (using three feet as an example of a theoretical colon):

three struck syllables can rise toward a peak-accent; they can descend from a peak-accent; they can rise to a peak-accent at the center and fall away; they can (though it would be practicable in very rare instances) fall along a level course, neither rising nor falling (this last would be monotonous—except perhaps if it sets up a powerful accent in another colon contingent upon it —and is what is often found in academic translations of poems, *cf.* verse translations in the Loeb Library series), etc.

But I want to stop here; this is too much theorizing without concrete instance. What I would like to do is examine briefly some passages of poetry in the light of my assertions.

It may be best to start with a passage from a poet who was often too much caught in the written word and not enough in the spoken word. But the passage I take from Keats, the famous opening lines of *Endymion*, are amongst the most "oral" that he created. Unfortunately, amongst other faults, the poem becomes mere writing too soon and only occasionally rises from the page. However.

---

*"Colon" seems a useful designation, to me, because it suggests a linkage and movement, as though it were the "leg" of motion, the motive element in a journey.

A thing of beauty is a joy for ever:
Its loveliness increases; it will never
Pass into nothingness; but still will keep
A bower quiet for us, and a sleep
Full of sweet dreams, and health, and quiet breathing.

Whatever there is of the trite in the words, the rhythmic and melodic structure of these lines lifts into an effective poetry. The academicians, and they are many, think that I dont know how to scan poetry, as though it required great insight to chop these lines into the feet and caesurae of rhymed iambic pentameter. But, though Keats very certainly had the academic measure in mind, he constantly leaves it behind in the exploitation of melodic structure, in this passage. Part of his ultimate failure is his leaning too heavily on the old prop; he ends up merely filling empty space, empty time. But here, as analysis in oral terms reveals, he breaks his structure with great *affectiveness*.

I find that these lines hang on triple-phrasing. I would break the first voice accordingly into:

A thing of beauty   is a joy   for ever

and follow the lines this way:

Its loveliness   increases;   it will never
Pass   into nothingness;   but still will keep
A bower   quiet for us,   and a sleep
Full of sweet dreams,   and health,   and quiet breathing.

(The simplest test of my accuracy is to read the lines according to breath; I think you will find that my phrasings permit both a natural and an emphatic movement in the lines without straining the lungs; in fact, I think you will find the movement a pleasure to the breath.)

Put somewhat baldly, and keeping in mind that it is a simplification, it is accent that creates the basic rhythm and quantity (timing and sound-values) that creates the melodic line; but both must cohere in a true poem. Accent is the dance; quantity is the song.

As is evident, Keats wrote this poem using the ''line'' as his basic unit of structure, his conscious unit of structure; but his ear, his voice, combine to assert a strong melodic structure that sustains the much-modulated base rhythm. The opening line builds on a passionate rising rhythm that levels off to create a tone of quiet exultation. "Thing" is a simple mounting accent in the first colon, the breath saving itself to strike the first syllable of "beauty." The second colon, after a comparatively long breath, rises with urgency toward the rich diphthong of "joy" hardly pausing on the preceding monosyllables. The final colon in the line takes its pitch from the height of the word "joy," and though the soft "e" of "ever" would not normally be capable of bearing such stress, it maintains the precedent pitch before sighing off (a melodic waver) and suggesting the quieter modulation that picks up in the next line and is maintained, lengthening out, in the next verses of the sentence.

Two final observations may be made in passing to these verses: first, that the lengths of the lines (quantitatively) obviously vary, so that to say "iambic pentameter" and think by that to have described the structure of the poem, is pure nonsense. Secondly, the rhyme-structure of these verses (not necessarily the case in all poems, nor even throughout a given poem) provides pause in every instance for the breath to regather, though the lengths of the pauses vary according to intensity; i.e., the pause at the end of the first line is the longest of those quoted and accommodates the delayed accent of the next line (which also is a modulation-shift) in contrast to the struck opening syllable of the following line.

To move from Keats to William Carlos Williams is to move from the nineteenth century dramatically into the twentieth century. Immediately you sense a language less pinned to the page, a language that picks up from speech: the prose line has entered the poetic consciousness. And it is perhaps of the utmost importance that it does not evaporate.

I select Williams quite simply because he is outspokenly oral in his manner and has made a break with past structures a programmatic part of his work, and because of his present concern with measure. In his work before *Paterson* Williams consistently broke "faith" with the line, as in fact had Hölderlin and Rilke before him. His attempt has always been to keep rhythm open and not to use lines as compartments of rhythm, somewhat isolate one from the next. But it is clearer now that he has not at all abandoned linear structure. Certainly, though he broke it open, he never did abandon it. But what is the sense in having lines, unless

70

they are used; unless they function? It is as bad as any empty convention of form. Or why have stanzas? (As he so often does.) I do think that often his structures are dull and ineffectual. But when he lets his voice carry and the rhythm rises to the occasion, he draws his structures much more intimately into coherent play.

But I want to consider here one of his later poems for the light it sheds on his more conscious structural practise today. I think it demonstrates certain possible developments. The poem I have in mind is *The Yellow Flower*. The first stanza (or paragraph) runs as follows:

> What shall I say, because talk I must?
>   That I have found a cure
>   for the sick?
> I have found no cure
>   for the sick   .
>   but this crooked flower
> which only to look upon
>   all men
>   are cured. This
> is that flower
>   for which all men
>   sing secretly their hymns
> of praise. This
>   is that sacred
>   flower!

To try to analyze the structure of this poem by any conventional system of metrics is doomed to failure or all kinds of rationalized licenses. We could pitch it into iambics and anapaests, since the rhythms are rising ones. But I want to know first how Williams sensed the structure and then examine in detail what the structure really is, or is not.

To start with, the line (triple-phrased) is the conscious poetic unit of development. These lines, for example, are much truer *as lines* than the quoted lines of *Endymion*. They stand sensibly as lines. And they move as lines. But what determines them? Not accent (under any interpretation). Not the sense of an underlying iambic pentameter (as John Ciardi wrote in review not long ago, picking up the subject, not without point, of Dr. Williams' metrics). There is the breath, clearly, and the ear.

But just how are breath and ear used in the structuring? (It should be noted that no discussion of metrics can get very far, if it assumes that this or this is how the poet ought to be shaping his work. Honest examination, not wishful thinking, should be the base of attack. And open sympathy. Whether one likes the poem finally is not at all unimportant, but it is less important in this matter than concern for poetry.)

I find that each fragment of a line represents a drawn breath, with this emendation: that every point of punctuation marks another breath taken; so that, say, in the first fragment of line, the comma indicates two breaths are involved. It is fair enough, then, to ask why the poet doesnt break this into a more apparently consistent pattern. It seems to me the reason is simply that Dr. Williams wants to draw the maximal advantage of linear structure, however much more ordered the breath-arrangement has become in these more recent poems; i.e., there are the values of sense, of emphasis, of intensities, of the melodic lines. The rhythm assumes gestures.

Because the tone is more markedly conversational, not overtly musical as *Endymion* is, the accents are more broadly spaced, the rhythms are marked by phrasal repetitions. Certain sounds carry the melody and reinforce the rhythmic succession: "talk," "sick," "sick," "crooked," "look," "secretly," "sacred," modulated by the repeating "cure," "cure," "flower," "cured," "flower," "flower." The recurrences of "found"— "found" and "all men"—"all men," plus the pointing of "This/is"—"This/is," create what is a comparatively straight- forward elaboration of speech-rhythms, using the excitations of the breath as its evolutionary force and the ear and the eye as line- surveyors. The peculiar (idiosyncratic) use of the non-syntactical period (.) in the middle of the second line is an innovation of Dr. Williams (though it has parallels in George, Pound, Olson, etc.) and functions as a dramatic pause, throwing a stronger accentu- ation on "this crooked flower," which moves on to become "This . . . sacred flower!" at the end of the introductory stanza.

Several important matters rise out of all this analysis. I think it is clear that a poetry orientated from the spoken language opens immediately to an infinitely complex rhythmic structure where accents occur with less marked regularity and where various melodic tensions are needed to hold the structure in. Also it

72

becomes more and more essential that linear structure, the placement of margins, punctuation, are refined in practise, since such a poetry requires the aptest precision, or it falls dully apart.

We have been so long accustomed to cyclic form that it is hard to believe finally that any other structure exists in poetry. But the structure of a poem is essentially serial, though no unit discards itself at any point. What has happened at any point informs what is about to happen and what is happening refers both back and forth. To diagram the action of a poem is to evade its contingencies. It moves: everything that happens in it is contingent. To create is to create structure. To limit structure therefore to the circle is to miss the point. It depends on how you want to see structure. Lay the circle flat on its edge and you have a line.

I am inclined to think that our speech rhythms could do with more tensing in many contemporary poems. It need not be made into a steel trap, as Hopkins tended to make it; it can be left open and flexible. Of course, certain voices, if we are attentive and become familiar with them, like Pound's or Williams', can accommodate a great deal of low-pressure verse in longer structures without necessarily boring us—though it is debatable how long the muted accents can hold us. And I sense amongst the younger poets today a development, whatever their allegiances, towards tighter rhythms and more marked accentuation. Speech has such possibilities on which to ground a poetry.

3. *The Structure of the Oral Poem*

It is interesting to set against Blackie's comment on how Greek and Latin poetry should be read, what the elder Yeats wrote of son Willie (1884): "His bad metres arise very much from his composing in a loud voice manipulating of course the quantities to his taste." But then, this is what every poet does; if not every reader. The difficulty lies in the poet's notation of melodic and rhythmic intent.

Now the oral poem has the problem licked at this crux. It is itself the poetic event, the precise thing, the very make of the poet, where no interpretation vocally is needed. It brings the poem that much closer to the potential recipient.

At all times the poet has tried to use his written structure, the visual device, to underline and clarify his rhythmic and melodic intent, and in our time a great deal of development has occurred (as Olson acutely points out in his *Projective Verse* essay) through the use of the typewriter, where marginal dispositions are conveniently available and spacing is so correct—though we may not have the huge "canvas" that Mallarmé's *Coup de Dés* requires for its constellational structure. So that, although Cummings, say, cannot precisely demonstrate how he wants his poems read, he can do so with previously unexploited accuracy: as,

in Just-
spring when the world is mud-
luscious the little
lame balloonman

whistles   far   and wee

and eddieandbill come
running from marbles and
piracies and it's
spring

when the world is puddle-wonderful
the queer
old balloonman whistles
far   and   wee
and bettyandisbel come dancing

from hop-scotch and jump-rope and

it's
spring
and
   the

     goat-footed

balloonMan whistles
far
and
wee

There was a time when this was considered mere eccentricity or cuteness; it has long since become evident, I hope, that the layout of this poem is strictly set for vocal presentation (apart from the use of, or non-use of, capitals). Space is punctuation. And yet, to hear Cummings render this poem is to realize that the dimension of his voice is not wholly written down. He creates pitches and persuasions that cannot be noted down structurally; they are in the event of the voice.

It may be thought that this becomes too "personal." I dont believe so. I believe that the individual voice, as voice, has its proper place in the make of poetry and it ought to be precisely present. Also, the oral poem is always the poem present. It is never a past event. It never permits itself to be considered simply intellectual fare.

But this gets away a little from my subject here. Let me copy, as nearly as I can, the words of an oral poem that I made some months ago, one of a series; it is the 3rd in a group of associated pieces.

I want to get
out
to rise
out of
          my self

There is
that other truth
that is not
my
     self

But your tongue touches my tongue
and kills me

And knowing death
I know nothing else
and I can say
               nothing else

but—

<pre>
        "Death
  be
      my
          breath"
</pre>

What is clear, I think, is that in the oral poem the breath (being used as a contemplative unit) elongates key syllables and creates, often on resourceful diphthongs, a carrying beat and music. The lines, as I note them, are fairly accurate indications of time, of quantity. And quantity assumes an extraordinary value in the oral poem. I have no way of precisely indicating the length of the word "Death" as it falls at the close, but no reader would be likely to approach my expression of it.

You can see, at least, how the structure mounts itself upon the struck syllable and the length of the breath, how the voice will linger on its springboard and then leap. But how put down in writing the intensities given each word and the unrepeating modulations that give harmony to a comparatively simple written structure? And you see, or learn, how word leads to word and phrase to phrase, that alliteration is such a natural element in organizing poetic thought.

I wish you could hear this as it is given, to understand, to experience, how different a thing it is from its written counterpart. A total intimacy exists. And it is true.

The mystery and the mastery of the voice, as it finds itself, as speech discovers its rhythms, as the mind makes shapes, leaps to shape, shines, out of what is happening from the mouth, out of the breath, is entire. There is the need of imagination and its rein; there is not the dispersion of it or over-careful disposition of it in analytical revision and the self-martyred intellect, only the known vision. (Lorca calls it "duende.") And needless to say, the event is dramatic at base. As speech always is, when it is truly dialogic, aware of the other. Self addresses a variety of selves. More than "addresses"! Enters into relation with. Hearing itself, it responds to itself; sensing the other, it throws out "lines"; it draws the other in, to antagonize or protagonize, agonize: to feed and to feed on, to grow, create, mature.

Paris, August 6th, 1955

(from *Origin,* 1st Series, No. 17, Fall-Winter 1955-56)

Oral Poetry

. . . as they had delivered, both in time,
Form of the thing, each word made good and true,
The apparition comes. . . .

Hamlet

Who heareth, seeth not form
But is led by its emanation

Ezra Pound

What one comes back to inevitably, as I do here, is the ear and the voice. If it needs saying, I dont take either as ''parts'' but as junctions with the whole nervous system known as human mentality.

Of the ear, as distinct from the voice, two preliminary discussions may be in order, to clarify certain slides in our time that seem to apply precision to the subject of poetry, but in both practise and fact confuse matters by their essentially inadequate fragmentation.

There have been many studies of metrics and such rhythmic phenomena by various acoustic machines and much data collected. When one such device has decided definitively for us that such things as ''syllables,'' ''sentences'' and even ''words'' dont exist, but only certain sound combinations, etc., it is time to arrive at a reckoning. The matter is clear enough. No acoustic machine can be compared significantly with the human ear. We are not guessing when we say that we recognize and hear ''words,'' ''syllables'' and ''sentences.'' Art is nothing without its psychic component, nor is human life. Instead of beginning our studies with the acoustic machine of the laboratory, we must begin and *stay* with the human ear.

Metrics, this other engaging phenomenon that has haunted critics, estheticians, and occasionally poets, has such a way of trapping one. In one's eagerness to find a measure, one invents a

77

measure and builds a more or less cogent system upon it. But the problem is both different and more complex. Karl Shapiro has frowned upon centuries of practise by "ear." Even Dr. Williams, whose practise is admittedly and obviously "by ear," finds the need for a measure profound, though he searches for a "variable" measure. Maybe I can simply undermine these efforts by asking you to try a very simple experiment—perhaps one that you have tried at one time or another—in rhythmics.

With a pencil or any handy instrument drum on a table certain counted and fixed rhythms. After a few minutes of this, gradually arriving at more and more complex counted patterns (according to one's deftness of hand and ear), one tires of the "counted" pattern. And it is not only the hand that tires of it. It is the ear as psychic element, as the attention. It is not very interesting. Now, just like that, forget about counting, MAKE RHYTHMS. You will find yourself perhaps thinking of certain songs. And what you discover suddenly IN THE PROCESS (during which the mind has remarkable fluidity and freedom) is that the ear is much more engaged, involved, and that the rhythms are incredibly more complex—seemingly WITHOUT THOUGHT and certainly without any overt count. That is, the thinking involved runs either ahead or behind (in the sense of "at the bottom of") the rhythmic movement.

Now, clearly, many essential elements of poetic structure are caught up in this experiment. (I am not concerned here to focus on the strictly musical problems except as they reflect directly upon poetry.)

What I discover, without any advance bias, is 1st, that the ear, the human ear, is considerably more alive to nuances and control of them than any "mathematical system" we can rig. And, 2nd, and this is central, this very complexity is of such engaging richness (at least potentially, if not in fact) that one feels time concentrate and in that concentration SHAPE. Mathematics is a logic that implies its entire "rhythm" or development *a priori*. But art is not *a priori*; it is not such a logic. It is the entire of concentration of one's mean upon the instant and, if it comes off, it creates a fulfilling presence.

There are many other facets that the experiment implies and suggests, but I want to hold strictly to this central notion and get it clearly across, beyond dispute, that the ear is not a *primitive*

78

device, no more than *Ugetsu* is primitive drama (though we have an inordinate tendency to mark down as such either what is exotic or, what is nearly the same finally, what we do not understand or comprehend). The ear, and the voice for that matter, the whole mental structure of man, is of a fineness that we dont even begin to appreciate—though every so often physiologists or anatomists tell us so, from their somewhat mechanical points of view. In short, no metrics we can devise, no variable measure, will ever be so sure and so fine as the ear and the voice are and can become.

Before I move off these points to oral poetry and its mesh with them, I might pick up the response of someone like Dr. Williams, who probably would agree with what I have said and still say that we must understand more perfectly than my generalization the nature of this fineness of ear and voice. I dont disagree, and here science MAY be useful—provided it doesnt catch itself, as it prefers to do, in such partial analysis as loses any possible contact with the intrinsic life of the creative act. We begin to rely so much on equations and their finalities that we no longer see anything, but let the symbols see for us—which is only a more abstruse form of highpowered journalism, that is, organized blindness. Maybe I can put it more positively: I think the best we can do as critics and as poets is to refine our whole mental possibility and that means incessant practise. Which doesnt mean "down with thinking." Quite the contrary: it is apparent I hope to everyone by now that art is the most concentrated form of "whole-thought" man has come upon, discovered and explored. And it is the only mode we so far have found that breaks through the "logic-barrier." It is the greatest velocity the human mind can apprehend.

OK. I simplify. I do so, I risk doing so, only because poetry as I think of it is not a theory, but a presence. And its presence is readily available for those who have sense for presence. (You will sooner or later, as you think what I have said over, realize how all this ties in profoundly with notions of time.)

Now, I have listened to many arguments against "oral poetry" (which I have explained in more detail in previous numbers of *Origin*). And I have conjured up more, as I have thought more and more about it. But the one thing I cannot *argue* is its power. This is not a theoretical issue any longer. I have created such poems, i.e., directly, without rehearsal, onto wire (though tape, if I had had it, would have been better, for technical reasons only). I agree that such poems can degenerate into mere psychoanalytic performances or surrealistic rites (though it would be rash to leave it at that, since both these modes have relevances to the poetic act and I cant, like Valéry, for example, dismiss them with a certain hauteur). I agree that such poems can flounder and flop. But there is no need to keep such failures (except as "exercises," for one's own study) as "poems." Valéry also has maintained, with open debt to his master, Mallarmé, that "first thoughts" are usually of only germinative value and he would scarcely accept them as "finished products." And I take Valéry seriously, as the most finished exponent of the "traditional" point of view, buttressed by a scientific clarity and patience of mind. But I cant dismiss Shakespeare because he "never blotted a line," though I too might wish he had—though not at the expense of several of his last plays. One of the side problems, but one which diverted Valéry so much, was the problem of immortality via poetry and he concluded that if one made a fortress of a poem, that perhaps would do the trick. Fortunately, he could practise beyond his logical brilliance and could find himself in poetry. But it is a moot question whether Valéry's poems are more profound than Shakespeare's or Homer's. The profundity of poetry is not the profundity of logic. It is hard to say, but I think he tended to write poems for the classroom too often, though it was hardly his intent. Or maybe it would be more accurate to think of them as experiments with only the imagination as variable and even that severely limited by constants of form and language. But my remarks on Valéry are not at all definitive and he resists any easy dogmatism, I'm happy to add.

My point in this is merely that "the single shot" can find its target. In its very firing. It means that gradual refining of ear and voice that I have already mentioned. I refer you to the version I have made of a surrealist experiment by Artaud and Breton many years back, which appears in this issue.* I'm not interested in the futile discussion of its "greatness," but in pointing out that just any two persons could not have produced this very poetic correlation. In short, apart from what each poet reveals of himself

---

*See "Dialogue in 1928," printed as an appendix to this essay, p. 82.

in his responses (which is remarkably considerable) concentratedly, one senses beyond dispute poetic intelligences. So that though this performance is, yes, accidental, it is not random. And it is quite surely not chaotic or disorderly. For what is certain is that any man who lays claim to being a poet thinks entirely and substantially in and through language and when he can concentrate his fire in it must create a presence, which is the poem.

The advantages of the "oral poem" are manifold. I hope I have previously given a fair idea of them. But I briefly remark some again.

The oral poem keeps its fire right on the spot, where it belongs, in the poet's mouth. It brings into play such intensities as the written word, as such, cannot engage. Durations that on the page would seem like mere eccentricity, and would only approximate intent at that, become . . . become? ARE the very breath and root of the poetic act. The syllable is where the breath and/or the mind breaks off sound psychically as well as physically. Rhyme and all the devices of consonance are not superfluities, but the very steam of motion, the leverages that are needed, not for mere attention, but for the breath to find itself, for thought to be discovered and to leap forth. One discovers that a poem is never a dead thing, but moves like a fish in water or even a fish out of water in the hand, striving for its wholeness again. Its element. Clothed in its own element, its final filament.

The oral poem brings the poet back to the root of his act, speech, and to that drama that is in and of it, the debate that the self picks up within itself as soon as the mouth opens and utters sound, which assumes meaning. Consider, I can say "death," but the very timbre of my voice may say "life." You will say, it is "acting." Yes, it is acting, but the actor is the entire maker and the involvement and involution, the concentration of the act, is an ultimate motion. You will say, but then it is mere emotional excess. Yes, it is—as much as any work of art—but that only tells a fragment of what the act is that is going on. It is drama, droumenon, that runs on until its presence, its idea, is fully *realized,* and that's it. And it can lift you out of your chair or bring you down out of it, as though you were in the presence of a god. For you are in the presence of a god!

You will say, but if all this is true, why do you stand alone? Where are the others to make such poetry? We want to hear it. *I*

81

want to hear it. I cant speak for the others. I say the possibility now exists to make such poetry as can stand the world on its human feet. I will speak my piece. Let those who can and who care do likewise.

August 23rd, 1956
Matera, Italy

(from *Origin*, 1st Series, No. 20, Winter 1957)

Appendix:

DIALOGUE IN 1928

Question? Reply. A simple job of adequation that implies all the optimism of conversation. The thoughts of the two interlocutors are separately pursued. The sudden relation of these thoughts imposes upon them to effect a very coincidence in contradiction. On the whole very reassuring, since you love nothing so much as to question or to reply, the "Cadavre exquis" has executed to your intention some questions and replies whose desire, carefully unforeseen, is also wholly guaranteed. We are not opposed to what certain anxious minds see in it as more or less sensible amelioration of the rules of "scribble" games.

Antonin Artaud and André Breton

A. Has surrealism always the same importance in the organization or disorganization of our lives?
B. It is mud, in whose composition hardly anything but flowers occur.

A. How many times do you think you will love still?
B. It is a soldier in a sentry-box. The soldier is alone. He looks at a photograph that he has just drawn out of his wallet.

A. Has death an importance in the composition of our life?
B. It is time to go to bed.

B. What is immortal love?
A. Poverty is no vice.

A. Night or abyss?
B. It is a shadow.

A. What is it that disgusts you most in love?
B. It is you, dear friend, and it is I.

82

Speech: As It Falls: Is Poetry
(more notes on oral poetry)

> *A word is dead*
> *When it is said,*
> *Some say.*
>
> *I say it just*
> *Begins to live*
> *That day.*
>
> Emily Dickinson (1872?)

Much too slow is it dawning on some that hearing is far more acute in man than seeing. As a poet friend today remarked on hearing me say this—of his newborn baby—Already we draw meaning from each cry and grunt and breath.

The spoken word—if it is unrehearsed—if it is given, as it usually is, to event, to occasion—is and must be poetry. It is of an economy of force that is operative with a constancy that no other form of human address has to offer. And it doesnt—that is the essence of its economy precisely—negate the other senses, but rather evokes them more. A little reflection tells us that we see more with hearing/saying than with our eyes alone and at a depth of vision that sight alone cannot procure. Indeed, we have to turn to the finest painting and sculpture and architecture to approach equal possibility.

But speech is of an overwhelming immediacy. And it penetrates with a more coherent intimacy than even music, for we know the faces of speech better than we know musical combinations.

In fact, speech is not only OF body, it is our most intimate form of relation. But, and this is a point that warrants stressing, it is neither separate from the body, nor does it transcend the body.

In 1954, in Paris, with a wire-recorder lent me by the American Fulbright Commission—all that they had at that time, I recorded my first improvised poems. (My first essays on ORAL POETRY date from that experience and that, without any prompting on my part, they should suddenly be referred to by younger people, when they went unnoticed almost completely at the time, is an omen I can hardly ignore.)

It may be worth being explicit about what I mean by ''improvised poems.'' The poems are immediate: they are not planned in advance and there is absolutely no text. Naturally, I am thinking of poems all the time and the improvisations are likely to open from some already well mulled base. But the moment the machine is in motion there is no time to reflect—except WITHIN event. And I must be prepared to accommodate the accidental— whatever chance sounds may enter or visual recognitions, etc. I usually project—and it is a sudden decision—a sequence—of five or ten poems—not too many or I may forget and have, as a matter of fact, in longer sequences. And, of course, if I should feel so prompted, I could exceed the stated limit. But I take the limitation as an extra tension and ground: it compels a more acute concentration.

The poems have, as it happens, NOT been revised in ANY way and NONE, as it happens, have been erased. For, in such poems, there can be no ''mistake'': error is an active component here. It is always likely and always pertinent.

Those poems, again as it happens, made in Paris, for one reason or another, remained unheard by me until a month ago. Perhaps the extended interval, during which my work had undergone considerable metamorphosis, was salutary. In any case, it meant ''distance'' for cooler judgment. (At the time when they were made, my initial impression was one of startled elation—for I felt that something decisive had occurred, accidentally on purpose, you might say.)

The re-hearing, after so many years, was far more startling and elating, for the poems had not lost any of their original force, but in addition they carried for me a total recall of the scene—to textures, smells, physical space, and psychic condition. Certainly the most vivid recall experience of my life.

It reminded me of my first aural shock. At the end of World War II a brief recording made by a childhood friend who was killed during the war was played by a mutual friend. The voice was of such stunning accuracy and intimacy that I could hardly breathe: the effect was almost TOO MUCH. The vivacity of the boy was wholly present again and his absence took on such relief as to make me wonder what "spirit" might be.

2

As a result of hearing the old recording—rerecorded some years ago by a friend onto tape—I have started again at improvising poems, but with the chance of greater extension—with my own equipment and with more time for it—I mean to push it along the solitary vocal arc as far as possible—without any technical trickery.

Then—when I feel I have reached the limit, my limits, of working alone and "straight"—I want to improvise with a small audience—a few friends or maybe just one other person. And this can be done also, to some extent, with distances between. Then with large audiences. Then various technical possibilities can be brought into play—but with very careful consideration of what each "device" means or may mean in terms of the event.

It may be realized, even by those of you who are unfamiliar with the experience, that to improvise poems alone in the face of the machine is, in a sense, THE human situation par excellence. The machine, going, imposes a TIME that is no longer that of the clock though it is strictly sequential, serial (if you will). And the time is one of psychic tensions, geared both by the going machine and the human capacity of expression.

It may seem sometimes like "acting," for it is clearly a PER-FORMANCE, but it is "theatre" of such painful intimacy that it moves well beyond that "theatre of cruelty" Artaud envisaged.

For the listener it is as if his own heart were become articulate: the meaning of what man is is brought home with an accuracy that cannot be evaded.

3

Whether the poems I have made would be paralleled by others improvising I cannot know—but I would suppose not. My improvisations are bound to reflect the nature of my own poetic preoccupations and the modes that are their expressive outs. The grace is that a man is suddenly allowed the opportunity to address others from his own most intimate depths without any drapery and in the fulness of his intelligence WITHIN OCCASION.

No improvisation can ever be repeated. It is ONCE essentially and vitally. The words can be copied onto paper and annotations of the voicing provided: I have tried this and published—in 1955— some of what was possible. But there is no annotation either fine enough or economical enough to state the event—assuming it were worth the effort. I did what I did, then, since it was such a novel experience and some sort of projection of it was necessary, if others were to get an idea of what it was all about. Even so, the little response I had—indicated my failure to get the experience across. With the much larger circulation of recording units and the increased interest in such media, the sense of what is involved is likely now to spread more rapidly. And be more understood. And —hopefully—realized.

Obviously the thing can be FAKED and the tape can be used merely as a device to catch spill from drug experiences or as a psychiatric extension of confession, etc. But the act of poetry remains constant: a sense of the other is inherent in it. Not as one to be impressed, but as one to be MET at the most profound level possible—that is, from the fulness of my being to the fulness of his.

4

The voice is an extraordinary instrument. And it is one that is intrinsic to human excellence. Every human sound has meaning for us. Music is relatively vague in comparison with ANY language and that vagueness is a very active component of its attractiveness and power—for it mutes judgment. Speech, in any of its forms, engages us with an almost terrible precision; it is so strictly provocative.

As children we had plenty of occasion to turn to the jingle:

"Sticks and stones
    Can break my bones—
    But names will
        never harm me!"

But the very need to resort to the jingle, as a taunting comeback, tells how much deeper than bone words wound. Or a poet's young son in Montreal, when I was once walking him to school and two classmate girls went by and made teasing cracks about the size of his ears, which turned a healthy crimson, muttered to me: They dont mean anything to me, such words— but why (he pleaded with me!) do they keep ringing in my head?

Why indeed!

Language is our medium. And it is weapon, instrument, plume and rapier, bomb and caress. It is the soul and spirit that we extol ourselves by. It is the exaltation and exultation man has provided himself out of his physical being. It is a bond.

5

The voice of the poet, the genius of language, he for whom words are substantive and always renewable and renewing, his nourishment to receive and to offer, as it finds its way out immediately onto tape, out of the depths of the plight in which it finds itself in him, cannot fail to touch at once every listening heart. It evokes the man of man. It says—with love—we are inextricably a single soul.

If my suffering and my joy cannot contain yours, then I am too small for even your smallness. The larger breath awaits to close upon us all.

I say listen, mean speak.

We share one silence.

(from *Origin*, 3rd Series, No. 11, Oct. 1968)

The Word as Faith
(more thoughts on oral poetry)

A Word that breathes distinctly
Has not the power to die . . .

Emily Dickinson

Perhaps we have foregone the living word so long now that we have forgotten what and how taking its power is.

The utterance cleared in the religious poems of Donne and the drama of Shakespeare eludes the actor who does not *live* (= love) the speech provided. And there has been little enough since, alas, that has moved or been sprung from equal depth, from an equal involvement, equal sense of risk.

But what remains is and is more than a little, and continues to be more. Only we need renewal, a fresh contact, contagion, in "terms" of our own moment—as to feel again what it is that stirs in what is given, that stirs us insofar as we are stirred, and rests.

1

The first experience at firsthand I ever had of professional theatre came at about age 14. With a group of young friends I had gone to see the popular film and vaudeville circuit comedian Joe E. Brown do *Elmer the Great*—a thin vehicle that allowed him to pull his famous faces, etc. We sat about as high as the angels go in such confines, so that the actor was miles away. But we had opera-glasses for the occasion and could see and hear enough. And the magic of theatre, as it always has with me, operated: the world that penetrated the world opened and we shared the romp.

We were, of course, content with what we saw. We had seen a

star; he had made us laugh. We were in no way edified, but we were pleased and that was what we had come for. (At that time, poetry was still almost a dirty word to me and I had virtually no experience to weigh against what was presented—except for short films, of very much the same caliber. In short, all judgment was muted.)

But when the play ended something unusual occurred— unusual certainly for me and sufficiently moving that I recall it now and have recalled it often—with warmth and a degree of pleasure that extends beyond anything that occurred within the actual play witnessed.

Joe E. Brown, after the applause for him chiefly, brought a chair out onto the proscenium and sat down before the audience— the lights "up." And then he spoke—to us. BEYOND performance. Of his career and of his sense of theatre. I dont recall that he said anything that could be called "profound," but he spoke quietly and with an evident regard for the audience. (And it was clear too that this was something he had done before and liked to do: perhaps even more than performing: "being with.")

I mention this incident because it made a lasting and strong impression on me; it "made" the occasion as the performance alone would not have. It reached beyond play into play. The comedian had realized that language was a power of intimate address and was willing to use it so.

I'm not sure it would have mattered what he said; his attitude and language, though trite, I am sure, were sincere. That carried. And yet at this further reach I know that what he said might have mattered far more again. But then he would have been another person, perhaps myself. Or you.

2

We cannot know, we dont know, how penetrating our words often are.

The finest poet I know advised me years ago when I was travelling around the USA and Canada and elsewhere reading his work to whatever audiences I could find that I was wasting my time, that no one would understand or follow.

For myself there has never been any doubt: the word is my

faith. Whatever man may mean to man is communicate through language and more in utterance than in the written word. The spoken word realized is renewal.

How do I know that in all the audience someone or some ones heard? I know as a mother knows her child's silences. I know as a mother's child. I have sat before poets and listened and heard. And as unique as I am is every other.

The word uttered from center touches center: emptiness sounding emptiness.

Nor is this pretty talk. It is what the heart corroborates, if it works at all, at every moment; it is what knowing is. It is that each man dies his death.

3

Fifteen years ago in a converted broom-closet near Notre-Dame in Paris I started making oral poems. That possibility was interrupted, for a variety of "reasons," until recently. But resuming it now I have re-discovered and I hope and trust that the re-discovery will open an entire antiquity, prehistory, of utterance that has so long been in abeyance.

For the spoken word, drawn to occasion and strictly shaped by it, has an immediacy, that is the necessity of all being, that makes presence pulse, feel, think, and indissolubly. It is why I have elsewhere said that the world as fully realized in speech is poetry. A poem, conversely, that does not say itself in you as your own speech fails as poetry, fails to be realized.

And realization always, in my sense of it at least, is more than an intellectual by-product; it is the event as complete occasion: oneself given to it, given to all else, which is never more else than one is. There are no asides and no digressions; there is no theme; there is only the living-dying going on.

Oral poetry, then, is not at all the written word, nor the gush and spill of some spontaneous composition.

Like the ancient calligraphy of an Oriental priest or soul, providing a text of event for one who came to it for touch, the oral poem is not a commercial venture; it is a transaction whose profit does not exist materially, but in the begged spirit.

It occurs from need unto need.

I cannot imagine a world destitute of human beings who do not need love, in whatever form available, possible. Oral poetry, the words I find within myself at a given moment, within a relative repose, where as much of myself can come forth as possible, is made to meet such need. It is one self conversing with one self. If the words seem all on one side—monological—it is no more that simple than an audience listening to actors on a stage: the action is shared, the words are no more mine alone than my breath is "mine" when uttered.

4

We live only within event, within realization. To share life kindly is most difficult, for we are given to demand and imposition out of fear and denigration, out of imminent annihilation. We beg, as I say, a farthing of spirit to set story by, to cling to, to feel the "I am" has meaning, makes sense.

Oral poetry, as I subserve it, carves through this soft medium and reveals the air of which it is a part, perhaps least particle. It makes sense only as immediacy, as realization, as event, occasion, meeting.

The dialogue occurs within the hearkening. For whatever the words that have come to me within the utterance, as it goes on, are moved towards any other as presence. So that the oral poem, insofar as it is operative, declares immediately your presence as ineradicable and hopeless.

The words I begin are words of air, but good to hear . . .

Take this from the book of *Winged Words* held by Sappho on an Attic vase from about 430 B.C.

One man greeting another on the road may say Good morning and the other say Goodbye, but both partake of a meaning that is as inevitable as it is ineffable and that shares with the passing wind the slightest influence.

There is nothing so modern, or ever shall be, that will undo the quality of one human syllable whose cry holds still to silence the only flag.

11 October 1968
Utano

91

The Problems of the Oral Poem

The word, the unit of meaning in utterance, whether that be what we customarily think of as a word or whether it be a silence or half a word or a choked syllable or any other phase of utterance touching or reaching meaning, is the material and indeed theme of all poetry, but literally dramatically so of the oral poem.

I put it in so dense a way because it may easily be mistaken as the simplicity it is. That is, I want you to sense the intricacies of an event that must feel extraordinarily simple, immediate, direct.

Several charges have recently been laid against oral poetry by a friend who has had a little experience of it. And perhaps it is wise to consider the charges before they fester.

It has been charged that the oral poem, in its choiceless spontaneity, is likely to be incapable of bearing up over any stretch of time. Chiefly, the likelihood pivots upon the lack of care that would seem to be implied in such a mode. Now it must be granted that such work requires absolute concentration and awareness WITHIN the event. Inasmuch as the vast majority of written poetry does not endure, it becomes equally clear that care is not guaranteed through writing, nor even through extended revision. As for the literal physical possibility, it may well be that the tape-recorded poem will outlive the type-printed page (books as we now know them). The Vedic literature came down to us from remote antiquity without a syllable lost—orally. This, of course, does not mean that the poems were therefore never revised, that they exist now in the very first version that occurred; that seems to me unlikely in the extreme—though not impossible. We would have to know a great deal more than we do about the way poems were made at the time those poems were made to be sure. All that I would say here is that all of anyone's poetry is a single oeuvre and one poem revises what has gone before, picks up from precedents. Care and the gifts of language, sensitivity to speech, are always invoked—whether in writing or improvising "in the air." It is no more, and no less either, a matter of working in wind and water. But that's another matter.

It is said that the oral poem as against the written poem precludes the other as the imagined poet of the word. And that is true. The poem I utter remains uniquely in and of my voicing. The listener may, if he wishes, repeat my words with me—once he knows them from previous listenings—and no doubt that will happen in time, for various reasons, including parody; but for the most part, the listener WILL be the listener. But is *Hamlet* less to us if Shakespeare plays the role? Isnt there a keenness, acuity, of intention and attention brought home to us IN EVENT, that is of the profoundest use? The question is not quite rhetorical—for though I feel this is true, myself, it will need confirmation from others and to that extent the question is wide open.

The words of any oral poem can be, afterwards, copied off and roughly set down in some orderly fashion. But it is like Blake taking dictation from an angel voice. Only the roughest version is available of what is experienced as occasion. And it is impossible that anyone else should be able to repeat the original and unique event. BUT—and this is central—the fulness of the occasion resides in the meeting with each other, with each listener as a partaker of the "con-versation." The words of the oral poem find their counterpoint and harmonic life only in the ears of the attentive listener, the listener who truly enters the act. It is up to the oral poet in his poem and through it to meet ANY OTHER at depth and help educe him, educate him. And in that release know joy.

That it doesnt happen frequently in no way means that it doesnt happen or cant happen. But the only proof of what I say remains for listeners to-come to bring into being as their own responses, releases.

Actually the strength of both the written and the oral poem are fundamentally the same, though they vary in their delivery. Both live only where each breath of utterance occurs IN EVENT and is lost precisely there.

No poet who has not an adequate and a full feeling of utterance within the scope of his breath and throat can ever hope to make a strong oral poem—but this I feel is also true for the written poem, though the written poem may allow more "time" and can be presented in its most perfect form. Yet the most perfect form, for me, only occurs as unique event, as language given into event.

Such poems as I refer to are extremely rare, but they are unmistakable and unquestionable as event. They mute all judgment—like the passages between Lear and Cordelia in their grief-shattered final scene: this is the drama of life itself: the stage here is each man's, any man's, breath and it tells with utmost pang the nature involved.

To realize that one lives is poetry. And there is only the one theme of poetry—and this has always been the case—poetry. The oral poem so conspicuously and decisively returns the poem to the breath of which it is made that it brings the realization of living painfully home. Perhaps it is this nakedness, this immediacy, this address, that gives to the oral poem its responsibility.

Utano
21 October 1968

Continuing Oral Poetry

During my journey to America (from October of 1970 to March of 1971) recently I had my first opportunity to present my oral poetry to a wider circle of people than heretofore, to people who didnt know me or my work. And for the first time, and perhaps last, to a large gathering.

The experience was, needless to say, educational. For me at least.

I had made a cassette copy of my last two oral poetry tapes, so as to be easier to handle. One evening at the University of California, San Diego, in La Jolla, late in October of last year, I played the cassette recordings to about 35-40 students and faculty members assembled in a lounge.

The tapes take about an hour altogether. I provided a brief history of my work in this new medium and admitted it was all tentative as yet, since few had been exposed to it and it was hard for me via friends or myself alone to evaluate the material adequately.

The audience was attentive and quiet throughout.

At the end there were a variety of questions, laments, and comments. The following day a number of those present came to me individually and added more private responses.

Several clear points came out.

First, the oral poem is—in my practise of it—a highly intimate occasion and a number of listeners were embarrassed to be in the same room at that moment with so many others and in so well lit a

95

room. There was the feeling that the voice, so personally directed, should be heard in a room that was darkened enough so as not to be distracting and that there should be no more than a friend or two present, if anyone else at all.

Second, not everyone is prepared to listen. This may be true of even a prepared text, of course, especially if the work is being heard for the first time. Many of the older listeners, the faculty members in particular from the literature department, felt a need for a text in hand, so as to be able to follow, and, no doubt, check back by. However, one listener, a young woman in her 30s, in special graduate studies, was able, shortly after the playing to quote many sections verbatim. She told me privately, to my astonishment, that she had been deaf for nearly all of her life—since childhood, in fact—and had had her hearing restored, by new surgical procedures, only a few years before. She was far and away the most acute listener and since many of the poems dealt with listening, she felt peculiarly addressed by them.

One critic thought that I sounded like I WAS reading from a text and NOT improvising. This response was not in accord with any other, but it suggests that the slow thoughtful pace in much of the improvisation could suggest—in its reaching—a reading. Of course, in actuality the pace varied a good deal in the pieces.

Again, I felt moved myself by what I was hearing. And since my own experience, having heard the tapes a number of times now, exceeds that of any other listener, it became all the more striking that the words and voicing continued to hold fire, to remain fundamentally ''new''; that is, there was STILL an uncertainty involved as to whether the poems would find resolution.

Inasmuch as the poems are none of them resolved by some imposed conventional frame, or have any regular rhyme disposition, or any fixed meter, or indeed any clear predisposition, beyond that of communicating at depth and with extreme economy, this uncertainty may not be surprising. Even tho I know that the pieces all ARE resolved in one way or another.

This has brought me to the realization that the situation involved, the involvement in utterance, remains central. Utterance bound by consequential/serial ''time.''

René Guénon has quite accurately shown that ''time'' need not be read in merely quantitative terms and in music and poetry, for example, it becomes evident that "time" has at least three dimensions and is highly qualitative. And what is operating most profoundly is what is least open to quantifiable research.

Someone also felt that McClure's improvised verbal responses to animals at a zoo were more nearly the ideal of such an oral poetry. I doubt it. Oral poetry can be rather too easily turned into clever patter, humorous exclamatory matter or deliberate nonsense.

My effort—and it is not to be taken as a final paradigm either for me or anyone else—happens to be at this time, and from the start in 1954, predicated on a poetry that addresses itself to each other at the most naked and penetrating possible level. This is not a question of being confessional or shocking—which would be irrelevant—but of addressing myself from center to center.

Naturally enough, the way I phrase words, my rhythms, the words themselves, the themes, images, are always likely to be closely related to where I am at when I make the tape and that is, at least in recent years, likely to be very close to my written work.

Actually the earliest oral poems were far in advance of anything I was writing then. And I have often had the urge to write down some of my recent oral pieces and see if I can, by revision, improve them. But I have given up the task, since I have ample opportunity to write as much as anyone could wish and a good deal more, I suspect.

The third and final point that came through to me at this open session was when a number of the younger people, privately, said that they were dismayed when questions were fired at me immediately after the tape stopped. They had longed for a period of silence, even a few minutes.

I'm not sure of what this means, but I am sure it reflects an involvement that had thoughtful repercussions in them.

The oral poem is not a test for vocal interpretation; the vocalization and the poem are one and the same event.

Some people were disturbed and others gratified by the numbers that divided the poems, the numbers spoken in a rather flat manner. And finally someone asked how I REMEMBERED them—since the poems exceeded a dozen in each tape. I confessed that I had written them down at the time, for I wouldnt normally be able to remember them in my concentration.

How memorable the oral poem is is hard to say, impossible, in fact, as yet. For it would need many listenings. And whether listeners would care to undergo the experience frequently is another story.

The oral poem may be of interest for peripheral reasons, in terms of the poet's written work, in terms of how the voicing enters as part of a formal development of ideas/feelings.

I doubt if more sustained voicings of feeling-thought exist as yet.

In any event the event remains for me an open one and a place where one may speak to any other one with a directness that baffles understanding.

Utano
23 June 1971

IV. Prose

Beckett
(via his essay on *Proust* and *3 Dialogues with Duthuit*)

Beckett's essay on Proust is a remarkable one, brilliant in every way and it, in effect, sets forth all the central concerns of the budding writer with unusual clarity. That he wrote it by age 25 also tells the rigidity with which he has pursued the ideas that then obsessed him—as well as the stubborn integrity that implies. He has wavered in his venture—at least in public—not at all, so that his work has perhaps a greater consistency and, thus, density, within its scope than that of any other writer of our time.

That his two earliest essays that have had circulation were on two—more or less—contemporary writers, both working out of Paris and firmly in the European tradition (though both iconoclasts)—Joyce and Proust, suggests somewhat misleadingly perhaps a polarity that he tries to bridge and pass beyond. Both writers were exceedingly fine masters of prose style, refined personally as well and with unusual ranges of interest and with extraordinary linguistic capacity joined with extreme memories for the minute and local.

Beckett's work seems naked of detail in any comparison with the two "idols." Beckett is, if anything, a literary critic with a vengeance. He has ransacked European culture—and extended beyond as well (though at less depth)—to get at the weakness of the fruits in the face of modern hopelessness. He refuses every opiate—political, physical, artistic, religious—though well aware of them all. His own capacity is geared to speech and articulation and he attempts to work entirely from the bottom—not up and not in any specific direction—just "around." His comments on Bram van Velde, though very little related to the artist's work actually, reveal his own preoccupations, the most central of which is the inherent failure of all art in our time and that only out of the sense of failure can any art today proceed. It is decidedly anti-figurative, as a result, but also against all thematic approaches—including abstract expressionism. Beckett belongs to a classic stance that vaguely yearns for a more romantic position, but cannot bring itself to accept a solution that seems both too facile and too inadequate for the difficulties of the human situation. He is anti-logical, simply because of the neatness logic requires, and yet he is of a most logical temper and as a result is always advocating a cause for which he himself stands as negative witness! In sum, he realizes the complete inadequacy of his stance, but uses himself as demonstrandum of that inadequacy.

The essay on Proust lays down the vital commitments that Beckett has adhered to—at least until now. He often uses Proust as his own mouthpiece, but he selects only what has deeply touched him and his sympathy for the sentiments expressed is only too patent.

He refuses to burke dualism, assuming it—whether liked or not—as a given. His most positive convictions are of a negative order. Time—like Habit—is a monster. Indeed, he tends to equate them. He sees man as "victim and prisoner." "The good or evil disposition of the object has neither reality nor significance. The immediate joys and sorrows of the body are so many superfoeta-tions. Such as it was, it has been assimilated to the only world that has reality and significance, the world of our own latent conscious-ness. . . ."

It is clear enough, both in Proust and Beckett—and in Joyce too, for that matter—that this approach is strictly a one-man deal. And, indeed, Beckett underscores the issue frequently. It implies, of course, an absolute isolation and an impossibility, at root, to communicate. Yet all three writers are excellent exemplars—perhaps the most acutely successful of our time—of communicating what had seemed heretofore incommunicable. Taken together they constitute a depth of individual consciousness that is almost overwhelming in its capacity.

Yet they are all self-admitted "failures" in Beckett's sense of the word. They recognize the hopelessness of getting across and finally, naturally, the paradox of seeking endurance in the face of a palpable non-enduring nature: the mortal in search of the immortal, for a principle of meaning towards which to move (to gather one's energies, to devote oneself). All are seeking, in short, revelation, epiphany, illumination, lucidity, an absolute light, Tao. The only occasion is a hopeless transcendence. As Beckett repeats, via Proust, several times—the only Paradise is the Paradise which has been lost. He makes no bones of "the bitterness of fatality" and "the haze of our smug will to live," "our pernicious and incurable optimism," and we must admit—even if with chagrin—that Beckett himself has done his best to undermine optimism, and any smug will to live, as well as catching as many nuances of the bitterness of fatality for our delectation as one could hope to.

He, naturally, in the closet of self, in the skin of self, in the mind of self, the tightest contraption ever evolved, sees no way out —genuinely, "really." It leads him, as Proust, to: "whatever our object, our thirst for possession is, by definition, insatiable." Like Proust, however, he assumes that "love" is to be equated with the "desire to possess another completely." And he sees that Proust's work reflects the Protean impossibility of that. It follows that neither love nor friendship nor any communion is fully possible, nor—though he doesnt spell it out so clearly here—can one commune with oneself fully; only "commute" (as Durante might say).

That the personal plights of the authors involved cannot be abstracted from these Ideas Beckett doesnt get at—it likely would be thought "vulgar" by all of them. Nevertheless, in all of them there is a strong feeling of impotence at work. What Beckett calls "failure" might well be titled "impotence"—without entering psychoanalytical schemes to justify the term. The writing itself, then, and indeed all art in Beckett's terms, would be reflections, refractions, of that "failure," that fundamental "impotence" that reigns in human affairs. Needless to add, such an "attitude," and the word "failure" states an attitude, pivots upon consciousness, a critical consciousness, hyperacute, to the point of paranoia and schizophrenia, though the pseudo-medical terminology hedges the issue.

Art, then, is a form of masturbation. But, by the same token, Beckett could reply that *everything* man does can be interpreted as masturbatory.

The issue, however, is not so simple.

Beckett writes: "The creation of the world did not take place once and for all time, but takes place every day. Habit then is the generic term for the countless treaties concluded between the countless subjects that constitute the individual and their countless correlative objects. The periods of transition that separate consecutive adaptations (because by no expedient of macabre transsubstantiation can the grave-sheets serve as swaddling-clothes) represent the perilous zones in the life of the individual, dangerous, precarious, painful, mysterious and fertile, when for a moment the boredom of living is replaced by the suffering of being. . . ."

Beckett, as far as I know, has lived modestly. It would be inconsistent of him to do otherwise and stubbornness is the very pap of his work. Yet his work, like that of Proust and Joyce, operates out of a world—like that of Baudelaire before them—that is decisively "easy," "arranged." The bourgeois argument is not mine. Nor am I involved with moral judgments. Nor esthetic ones. Mortality is as much the hinge for me as it has been for every artist who has ever been worth his salt and that includes, certainly, these. (This is not to flatter myself, for the "hinge" or sense of it in itself guarantees nothing—but it is hard to take at depth anything that does not realize it as such.) In their desire, however, to set themselves apart—and their unceasing anguish—which is their only "theme"—they often fail to see or realize what virtually anyone with a modicum of sensibility does, who lives to age 35, say. And by "realize" I am not speaking of a mere intellectual stance—but of the transformation of experience into deeper more penetrated and penetrant possibility.

Habit, in short, is not a Monster. This is not an "Idea," as Beckett wants to believe, but another deceptive abstraction—whose quality is precisely to deceive. Habit or adaptation is a necessary ground of being. The very shape of our bodies is an illustration, exemplum, of habit, of adaptation. Habit, however, need not, should not, be a closed system. It should always provide a solid basis of "flexibility," point of departure. One doesnt ever leave "home," but only reveals oneself more there. After all, even in baseball, the object is to SCORE from homeplate to homeplate—to return, to be able to return, to where one started.

Beckett's diatribe against "habit" is strong and obviously fundamental to him. But he has set it up as a straw man and as such it is futile to defend, assuming it needs defense.

Beckett, to his credit, does not ease into mere self-indulgence as an answer to tedium and anxiety. He will wrestle with the intolerable. "The mortal microcosm cannot forgive the relative immortality of the macrocosm." He says. Whether it is true or not is a moot question, though at first glance it seems true enough. But it is hard for me to believe that Beckett hasnt seen through the sham of such a notion by now. There is enough implicit contradiction in the Proust essay to indicate Beckett would abandon this stance sooner or later.

One irony of Beckett's work, out of many, is that though he knows that logic wont serve, nor any programmatic illogic either, he escapes from neither. He speaks of the relevance always of the irrelevant, of how selectivity robs event of its trueness—yet he is by all odds the most abstracting of writers, for his approach is always intellectual (even when it "plays" the role of the simply "visceral") and "essential." Proust and Joyce made extreme efforts to project a total environment. It is clear that Beckett considers their efforts failures.

His approach is via the "involuntary memorism" that he puts at the center of Proust's achievement—from the initial madeleine flowering to a variety of other later sensuous openings forward and back. As a result nothing is offered "in detail" in Beckett's work PROGRAMMATICALLY, except what—in effect—crops up *in process*. He demands the involuntary. Just as he insists we break relation with "Habit," and deliberately forces us to lose all sense of "Time." (Other French writers have made the opposite, complementary, approach—oppressing the reader with precisely Habit habit habit, Time time time. Beckett's approach is unquestionably more difficult and more subtle, as well as more convincing.)

The brilliance of Beckett's reading of Proust is not my concern here, but his discussion of the sense of isolation, etc., merits attention from anyone interested in literate possibilities.

It all boils down to Beckett's own basic vision: "Suffering represents the omission of that duty (Habit), whether through negligence or inefficiency, and boredom its adequate performance." It leads him to say: ". . . the heart of the cauliflower or the ideal core of the onion would represent a more appropriate tribute to the labours of poetical excavation than the crown of bay." And he adds, from Proust: "If there were no such thing as Habit, Life would of necessity appear delicious to all those whom Death would threaten at every moment, that is to say, to all Mankind."

Beckett only tags along to repeat Proust's inadequate statement. He has only substituted, as Proust, a habit of his own for those of others and, not surprisingly, prefers it to the others— without making more than a "failure" of it even so. This is true of Beckett's stance, rather than Proust's. Anxiety is not the acme or epitome of life. There is a rhythm in life, or possible if not inevitable to it, that includes the habitual. Life is NOT necessarily "delicious" when one is threatened by death. Perhaps it was for Socrates, but I doubt if it was for many another. In any case, we can only tell from the evidences. Rembrandt's final portraits, etc., are not "delicious," but they are profoundly compassionate and more again than that: they reconcile one to the "return"—without concealing the aches involved. Proust is a dilettante of suffering, as is Beckett. They both have had the leisure to examine their aches and to dilate upon them for the edification of a human world that has enough ache without theirs—but they do edify and so achieve something that is utterly lacking from the usual self-exposé or case-history the literary scene is bogged in now.

It is decisively true ("Death is the mother of beauty") that the sense of dying, of personal death, provides the ground of every clearer chance given man. All our vision opens here, gapes here. We are made to savor life through such consciousness and ONLY so. Even as there is the tautology here that words conceal: for consciousness is the predicate of our physical dying.

Beckett labors and belabors the word "reality," which merges—though he doesnt realize it in this essay—with the notion of "significance." Anguish is real; joy is deceptive. He despises the body and fears it and yet derives from it the deliciousness of agony. Or simply ferrets out of the wretchedness a continuance that he has no desire to will to stop. And that in itself, if no great accomplishment, is still "something"; it is "real"—or so he thinks, so he wants to think.

Habit takes on the negative virtue of palliating "the cruelty of others" and the positive sin of degrading the individual. Relation can only be fortuitous and self-projected, lost in self. And he is acute enough to see that "At any given moment our total soul, in spite of its rich balance-sheet, has only a fictitious value."

(Sometimes his imagery and mental phrasings remind me of James.) He enters a description of what for him is the most brilliant of Proust's passages and which is a persuasive exposition of involuntary memorism. That such "memory" only can occur to one who has capacity for realization doesnt occur to him. I.e., Proust "connects" and continually arrives at fresh realizations, but very few do have such power of being. It is my conviction that only one who "habitually" questions the given, converses with it—which includes all one's own history, often to the least detail as leverage—but always out of a shifting ground, out of the fresh realizations, can reach such depths as come to Proust. And Proust himself, though mightily refined, leaves much to others. Beckett's realizations, unfortunately, are few and far between, for all the "purity" of his approach. It hugs itself too much and therefore has no chance to dance with others. It insists on "me"—even though impersonally.

The difficulty of all insistence is that it reverts to me me me. And Beckett's work is of an insistent insistence—whereas Proust and Joyce are beautifully varied.

(On the jacket of the book a photo of Proust that may or may not be intentionally comic, ironic—as if Proust were being levitated on his cane.)

Beckett sees the relation of Proust's hero with Albertine as a necessary degradation, as well as metamorphosis of affections. From illusion to illusion and then from disillusion to disillusion. Beckett prefers disillusionment for the reason that it is "not" Habit and because it is painful. He has a "faith" in the involuntary memory as being "absolute" (entire)—not abstracted —as being perfectly authentic, "real"—in brief: all that is given to man to be revealed. *How it is.*

He will push Proust to the point of: "all those that believe themselves loved are liars." But Albertine—like all of Proust's characters—and Beckett's to an even more palpable degree—is never independent—even at her most seemingly independent, but is an emanation of the author: is accepted and rejected as something imagined. This is, as always, playing God—but with the invariable conclusion for one who is reasonably honest that the role breaks down and everything dissolves into "fiction." Beckett makes a distinction between fictions and fictions, speaking of "artificial fiction" as that projection of the mind of another in

107

oneself. That the distinction of fiction and non-fiction carries very little water doesnt touch him. Dialogue, as Buber, above all, realizes, is impossible in such a situation. So it is that Beckett is all interior monologue ALWAYS. Proust and Joyce are, in passing, excellent mimics and can reproduce with alarming accuracy the verbal characters of others, but only as caricature, as highpowered mockery. Beckett is ''above'' this sort of thing and it is irrelevant to his sense of failure.

Beckett considers Proust's anatomy of the relation with Albertine as the *ne plus ultra* of ''love'' between men and women. Yes! And says: ''in the whole of literature there is no study of that desert of loneliness and recrimination that men call love posed and developed with such diabolical unscrupulousness.'' (Friend Creeley has tried to match the performance, but lacks the fastidiousness and intellect, not the intensity, of Proust. Proust always realizes something.) But Beckett never doubts that Proust knows all. That ''love'' in any profound or authentic sense is never involved in Proust's work doesnt cross his mind. For it would be utterly fatal to Beckett should love have any possibility. ''One only loves that which one does not possess entirely.'' Proust's epitome and Beckett's conclusion.

When he speaks of Proust's ''tireless crucible'' of mind, it well describes himself. Beckett exists as ACID. He intends to dissolve man in an acid bath, show the anatomy bare and then dissolve that too. ''The idea that his suffering will cease is more unbearable than that suffering itself.''

We return once more to mortality.

The idea of the dance, which is the only idea that can compass love, is entirely foreign to Proust, Joyce and Beckett. Joyce does have inklings of it—but his intellectual emotionalism doesnt let him ride it out. It stays clenched upon witticisms.

One cannot mitigate death or get around it, one can only come to it with a deeper commitment to it and therefore to others who must face it also in much the same conditions. Much more is shared and communicable than Beckett will allow. It is fear of loving that scares him from the possibility of being loved; it is the fear of responsibility.

The liberated female figure of our time has by and large only managed to be doubly damned. She cannot accept being a woman and the natural commitments of a single relation and she cannot accept her inability *not* to be a man—though she has renounced the female role effectively. (And she doesnt, oddly enough, expect men to abdicate their masculine roles. That would be unjust—for her desire is to beat man, as it were, at his own game. For some reason that has always escaped me. Freedom?) So our modern free-lance woman moves around with a paranoiac twitch, forever muttering at every man: Why does he look at me, the fool, as though I were a woman—or, excuse me, "just a woman"?

I mention the female plight because it is part and parcel of male impotence today—especially in advanced societies and the urban scene. Proust's relation to his father is almost superfluous—but with his mother—and grandmother—possession does seem to be at issue. Their devotion to him can be mistaken easily enough as possession. Most children eat their mothers raw and suffer lifelong indigestion as a direct consequence. Proust was no exception in this regard. In addition, the innocent, the pure, relation that attaches to childhood, especially when fully met, becomes in the sensitive child a morbid predisposition against the vulgarity of mere sexual relation. (The church is most adept and alert in making good use of this predicament.)

There is more than a hint of Catholicism in Beckett's reading of Proust and I dont believe it comes from Proust himself. Beckett is the inventor of a Do-It-Yourself Christ kit—a lifesize cross and honest-to-goodness rusty nails tossed in for good measure.

His reading of Proust is an act of affirmation of his deepest negative convictions (no others occur to him):

". . . if love . . . is a function of man's sadness, friendship is a function of his cowardice; and, if neither can be realized because of the impenetrability (isolation) of all that is not 'cosa mentale,' at least the failure to possess may have the nobility of that which is tragic, whereas the attempt to communicate where no communication is possible is merely a simian vulgarity, or horribly comic. . . ."

(This latter state of incommunicability is the hallmark of the dialogues with Duthuit—but whereas Beckett firmly grasps what Duthuit is saying, the latter is merely brought to a cry of absurdity and "get it over with, whatever it is you're trying to say.")

Beckett to this adds: (via Proust) "One lies all one's life long . . . notably to those that love one, and above all to that stranger whose contempt would cause one most pain—oneself." (It is a pity Freud didnt start from this text.)

He analyzes: "The only fertile research is excavatory, immersive, a contraction of the spirit, a descent. The artist is active, but negatively, shrinking from the nullity of extracircumferential phenomena, drawn in to the core of the eddy. He cannot practise friendship, because friendship is the centrifugal force of self-fear, self-negation."

This is precise, is accurate—but for Proust, for Beckett, by no means for all. Nor for all artists. But his running away from friendship is not fear? Is not negation?

Beckett exonerates all under the rubric of tragedy. "Tragedy is not concerned with human justice. Tragedy is the statement of an expiation, but not the miserable expiation of a codified breach of a local arrangement, organized by the knaves for the fools. The tragic figure represents the expiation of original sin, of the original and eternal sin of him and all his 'socii malorum,' the sin of having been born."

This is standard enough—but it is falling back on the old chestnut and does not suffice. There is no SIN, original or secondhand. No "delito." Unless innocence, the innocence of an infant, be considered "sin." There is clearly a plight—and because of it a desire to be able to be guilty SO AS to be able, perhaps, to EXPIATE that state of being. But being is beyond guilt—even though human being has nourished guilt, like its most cherished habit, to monstrous proportions. That Beckett should abet this Habit is suggestive of a Christian twinge that feels a little out of keeping.

Mortality, fatality, confronts us again. We keep coming back only because we cannot ever leave home base. We knock the ball, at best, out of the park, but only in order to come the more immediately home.

Innocence and ignorance deduct us all. Only gradually do all of us arrive at some sense of all that is provided us—and a rare few at a larger sense of it. Those few are invariably of a magnanimous spirit and find some mode of helping others to share that larger sense. To torment others with a sense of SIN is to bamboozle them even while beleaguering them. The dying is the precipitate of all human feeling and human being (even as it is for all that we call "living"). The blow of death needs dispersing and others are the invariable "solution" (in the physical sense of the word first).

He sees, as does Proust, the impossibility and contradiction of a stated "unity"—just like a man who insists that he is "humble" or the child shrieking—But I'm not yelling! Number has no relevance here and only ever for the analytical or referential mind of man. The situation is OF, the genitive case. And number is a meaningless and/or infinite predicate.

Dualism becomes equally meaningless—admit opposites, etc., and precision will bring you to the entirety of a gamut that comes full circle, compasses all—but only by reverting to a point radiating infinitely—much as light. Perhaps this is the "light" which Beckett gropes for in his comments on van Velde.

He comes round again to his involuntary memory theme and it brings him to state unequivocally:

"Reality, whether approached imaginatively or empirically, remains a surface, hermetic. Imagination, applied—*a priori*—to what is absent, is exercised *in vacuo* and cannot tolerate the limits of the real. Nor is any direct and purely experimental contact possible between subject and object, because they are automatically separated by the subject's consciousness of perception, and the object loses its purity and becomes a mere intellectual pretext or motive. . . ." But Beckett lets this boil over into a satisfaction that it becomes "real without being merely actual" and "the communicant is for the moment an extratemporal being." Beckett's resort to highfalutin language when downtoearth speech would suffice makes the matter suspect enough as pseudo-logic, pseudo-philosophy. Again he will not question the notion of "reality": it is an ingrained Habit. The column he clutches. The crutch he cannot do without. Ache. But if "reality," like "unity" is dispensed with—and one opens to condition, the OF, "surface" also loses meaning. For the fish—which is the top of the sea and which the bottom? Isnt there only the locus of his habitation? Where he lives and dies. One is never out of—just as one is always and eternally part of and interpenetrable, wholly, egregiously, penetrable. Not perhaps for such "intention" as man thinks he needs and wants. But beyond intention, beyond will, beyond desire.

In time or out of time, does it matter? Except as an individual will exacerbate his plight by seeing only himself, by recognizing no other. More apt would be to realize oneself ONLY as "other." For self is realized instinctively via open relation. Art (aspirate) puts the heart into what it touches.

111

He sees music as the catalyst in Proust's work, as the epitome of that which is "perfectly intelligible and perfectly inexplicable."

And if this is Beckett's ideal of art, I have no quarrel with him at all. He does, I think, revere art—even as he realizes it as a futile preoccupation; it rises above vulgarity for him and is as much a life as life allows; it is "the 'invisible reality' that damns the life of the body on earth as a pensum and reveals the meaning of the word: 'defunctus.' "

This purism, which again sounds only too tied up with religious structures, strictures, goes against my own grain, for I cannot accept any "reality" over against "the body." One is incorporate, whether definition is possible or not. The situation is so palpable as to be transparent, is itself "perfectly intelligible and perfectly inexplicable." What more does one want?

The only Paradise that is losable is the Paradise of being alive —aches and all. This calls for no explication.

What Beckett (from around 1949) has to say in reference to a trio of contemporary artists (Tal Coat, Masson and Bram van Velde) is largely reiteration of what he has already implied in the Proust essay. He extends his theme to painting, trying to point out—hopelessly—the inadequacy of Tal Coat and Masson, at least, insofar as they merely hope to emulate the old masters. Beckett is unvarying in his recognition that the situation has changed, that we can no longer—if we ever at heart could—accept "expression" as a possibility and yet to realize that we feel compelled to try to say something. In a sense he advocates an art of honest and unmitigated stammering. He finds, whether aptly or not (and he doesnt argue this point), that van Velde does seem to "admit that to be an artist is to fail, as no other dare to fail, that failure is his world and to shrink from it desertion. . . ." It is the realization that no terms are available to him that he can trust or confide in— and that whatever terms there may be that are worthy of his trust or faith are forever beyond his powers to know. It implies a faith in an undefinable irrationale.

Yet—unless it is "perfectly intelligible"—something clearly is off.

2 Sept 66

112

The Genitive Case

William Bronk's essay "Unwillingness, The Unwilled" (*Origin* No. 10, p. 59) tries to get at the plight that is humanly, consciously, ours—facing its evasions and clarifying them.

He opens with the question "What do we want?" This is deliberately ambiguous. The "want" is desire and need and lack. In fact, there is no question to be posed, for each of us is—incarnate—a response to an already rootedly elaborated situation. We are, because we were wanted: needed. Wittingly, or more likely unwittingly. (Though we dont, by any means, know all that we know.) Unique necessity—though a variety, infinite in effect, of uniquenesses was possible. "Unique," like necessity, loses meaning, like everything else, upon examination. But we know what we mean to mean.

What need was operative? The continuance of impulse. Dispersal of the blow. Space. Contiguities. We call need so constituted and individualized "self," but infer a personal reflectivity here—which, say, a table doesnt have, doesnt need. The table as such, the thing as such, the word, reflects our impulse, our motive, to be the god of the given.

In this impulse or selfness we find or feel relation to all that we regard as "organic" as self-evident—though we come to extend—through temporal degree—this impulsiveness to all "matter." The rock breathes. Mind you, the imagination leaps beyond conclusions. Is awareness.

Bronk faces and cuts through the dualism of self over against

113

all else in circumstance. This removes him to some extent from Beckett, who openly dogs the dualistic as unresolvable—Heraclitean virtually—in another effort of sorts to "face up," "fess up." The issue is one of limits of awareness.

Beckett admits and holds to the unsolicited but only-by-death-destroyed self, in all its panoply (intrinsic and extrinsic: which naturally includes history and other "ideas"). Accordingly, this self—sealed-by-personal-death—isolates itself, is isolated, from "all else," no matter how apparently interpenetrated.

There is another of all this that Bronk moves towards and that others, like Chestov and Bataille, jump at. It is a recognition that uniqueness is not a value, but a plight—and that it—for all apparent divisiveness—can (and with Bronk *does*) merge with, submerge in, the unlimited and unknowable. This tends towards a mystical stance, an ecstatics.

Bronk, however, is *not* a mystic. He is rather nearer Beckett in this—in not disregarding the isolate self, but at the same time, and this is the existential ache in him, he realizes that self is meaningless, for it evolves and collapses within some "frame" which not only isnt known but cannot be known and is itself the teasing hinge of all "knowing." (Ignorance insists upon thinking and so the labyrinth extends.)

Beckett also realizes the meanness and meaninglessness of self. It is less a nihilism than an attempt to *be,* beyond foisting transcendent meanings (values) upon being. Beckett senses the self (point-of-view) as unbridgeable alienation, Bronk as unabridgeable non-alienation. Bronk puts it plainly enough: "There is something which is and we are not separable from it."

We are thrown back upon ourself. The senses sense. We begin with—even as we close upon, clench upon—our own physical being. The psyche is the rat in the walls. And those of us who refuse to lie or shuffle realize that no ideas will excuse us from this plight. We are dying. And no one can die our death for us.

We insist upon "ideals" to conceal or dissolve or to make a way of and beyond death, to transcend the dust we are and are only more to become. We say our predecessors, in many instances, died that we might have a "better life"—but it is impossible for us or anyone to be sure that our lives are at all better for their deaths, since there is no scale that does not, by definition, falsify. Each life is unique and unmeasurable. Chuang-tzu's turtle dragging its tail in the mud makes mockery of our titles. Naturally, though, we want to have our cake and eat it too. That is only human. *Only* human? True, rather, of all that is living/dying.

This may, like Taoist thought, be regarded as an invitation to passivity, to some terrible conservatism—but every revolutionary has as his ideal a paradise—which is static. Every revolution intends to be the last one, like every war. But what man is ever anything but his own first and last? Perception shows us that we eat our cakes, given the chance, and are eaten too.

In short, "progress" can only be staked out in carefully delimited graphs. And this requires and reflects a stacking of the cards. Progress as such becomes another slogan, another part of the "pitch" to sell something. To sell man short.

The dying, then, as now, recurs to us as *the* instance and is more than mere idea. We put it from us in whatever way we can, or manipulate it. Bataille, as earlier mystics, would carve out an all-engrossing eternity that makes a joke of any one life, of mere self. It is a bath in nothingness.

Bronk could, I suppose, end up in such a wash—but so far has not.

Where I differ from Bronk is when he entertains notions like that of identity—though he does realize its limits—and of some power, even unknown, beyond us.

He addresses himself to the pseudo-issue of identity intelligently and realizes the pointless irony of it—the need for a uniqueness which is given whether willed or not. But what is involved is a rooted need in each of us to realize uniqueness and to let go of it. Most, if not all, are so put upon, as extensions of others (parents or their substitutes) that they often behave to "laws" they never much understand or appreciate. Not that such "laws" are either bad or inappropriate always or ever—but simply that they do not arrive through one's own capacities enough and obviate self. (There is a feeling of helpless absence, impotence, even as one acts.) The unidentified become extensions of those who play identity hard. (You are my emanation.) And think, or feel, thereby to assume command of destiny, etc. All that man has done or has happened to man (past present future) is less than a drop in the bucket, imaginary drop in imaginary bucket.

"If something wants through us," Bronk says, "if we are the instrumentality of a desire whose source is not internal, then to interpose our own will or personal desires is an avoidance of reality. . . ."

Bronk's use of the word "reality," like anyone's use of it, abrogates all issue; it acts as a polemical binder only and prevents touching down. What Bronk refers to, I think, is that any one's will is meaningless in the face of an unknown but all-encompassing will to which we are obviously given.

He moves from this into his telling affirmation: "If we are not to falsify life, but to have it for what it is, we must leave ourselves open to it and undefended, observant of what may happen, since our private will is not relevant, and we are not capable of apprehending or assisting any other will, and what we observe and feel is perhaps less will than being and the nature of being."

He answers this conjecture soon afterwards by noting: ". . . in experience . . . nothing is revealed to us of what our nature may be, or of what we must do. . . . We have supposed that there are wants and purposes but it seems likely that none exists."

By his own criteria, however, nothing we do, or dont do, can "falsify life." Whatever we do, or dont, is our life and there is no way to measure any falsification of it—unless we (as we tend to) set up limits within which to be true, etc. And, indeed, it may be said in reply to my previous comment on the pressures of identity that if a person, as it were, kowtows to and is submerged in another (in whatever way), that not only MAY be his identity, it IS. My point was rather one of possibility, more than of plausibility. It is enough to see the way each of us is, to see that there are countless ways each of us isnt. (The particular use of a book like the *I Ching* registers here. And perhaps the limiting corollary that life is, as each, particular in every part and quite uncircumscribable even as it is circumscribed.) Possibility is "real," known, only when it is actuality, occurs. We may say, and often do, that this or that MIGHT have occurred and we will agree that it WAS possible (say that Caesar didnt cross the Rubicon), but all the possibility is academic. Not false—for that is not at issue and only is when the game is properly set up. Philosophical dialectics here, if not always, confuse the issue, no issue at all, for what we go through is as clear as it needs to be.

Life is, in short, whatever it is. And being "open to it" is a polemical approach to sensibility that, drawn out from childhood, naturally "flowers," but more often being crushed or abused withdraws (turns upon and into itself) and comes to no more than a leaf here or there, a withered bud at best. Bronk is referring the private will, as it were, to the all-encompassing will of his own projection. Most of us are little concerned with any other wills but those of others near us and usually only as they prove unavoidably contingent. (TV, of course, provides extensive contingencies that often breed vague idealisms.) The water wont splash unless something MAKES it, at surface, jump.

What we must do is not "revealed" to us except through what we feel we are capable of and feel desirable and driven to do—which does, to some extent, if not entirely, come to us from beyond ourselves, but interactingly, and multi-dimensionally.

Bronk says: "We have supposed that there are wants and purposes but it seems likely that none exists." A mother feeding her child does not "suppose" the child's needs; she knows and feels them as her own. He refers more nearly, though, to some larger more inscrutable possible will or purpose.

He asserts that there is no need beyond ourselves driving us and then closes upon a recognition of the irrational emotional element (integrity?) within us that breaks forth as feeling and this, in all its welter, seems to him the most solid of all human experiences—"as though we were instruments a music were played on and we arch and turn to have the contact closer."

His closing image is a curious one in its metamorphosis, and ambiguous accordingly. First, the comparison to an instrument implies again some power beyond us governing us and moving us to its will, its purpose, which he has been at some pains to say we can know nothing of and can say nothing of. And second, he transfigures this into an animalistic figure that could be a cat—but the image is one of sensual foreplay—half agony half ecstasy or yearning: desire turning upon itself? The transfiguration, if realized as extension of our own physical nature, is more congruent.

And there can be no doubt that our feelings are dominant (pre-dominant) aspects of our being. They are consciousness replete. Consciousness, contrary to most philosophers since Socrates at least, is not by any means identical with or limited to "reason" or even "reflection" in any dialectical sense. It may well be a consciousness that moves beyond and through self-consciousness (which for man means reaching language).

Where do I stand in all this? Precisely where I am, where the

"I" and the "am" and all our positings are muted, transmuted, in event. At a point, a pointlessness, that neither judges nor can be judged. We live within an ignorance so complete and so hopelessly obvious that it affords us total asylum: it so denies anything but what we do know (bodies), which is what we feel and through feeling make. Make do. Nothing is, thus, denied—of history, or that construction we call "history": our interpretation of human being through phases of time in space and with varying notions of overarching structure determining same. Nor do I deny any imagining.

We are dying, Egypt, dying. Melodramatic, tragic, ridiculous, obvious. That is this. The very words here imply that continually and ARE as instruments of that fact and act and only. Livingdying. The largest commitment we know and are given to and must meet is the genitive case. We are OF. This is our predicament, our plight, our allegiance. We need not admit it; it doesnt matter a damn; we are OF—beyond choice, beyond faith. We are dedicate as we are. However we are. This does not translate out into meaning or shoot out into some order or ardor known as meaninglessness or nihilism, nor any -ism. It holds us where we are and releases us at once, as if the least breath contained, even as it does, the illimitable. Impulse is expulsion. Adam has moved beyond the grave: Eden is endless. The dying leads us by the hand; we savor the apple for as long as we can.

in epilogue:

Nearly three years after writing the above a new book of poems by Bronk appears (*That Tantalus,* Elizabeth Press 1971) and has a poem in it that perhaps can stand as his response to all that I have tried to say:

The Plainest Narrative

I am William Bronk, have been raised to believe
the personal pronoun plus the verb to be
and a proper name said honestly is fact
from which the plainest narrative begins.
But it isn't fact; it comes to this. Is it wrong?

Not wrong. Just that it isn't true.
No more than the opposite is true. That ''I''—
as arbitrary as the proper name, a role
assumed from the verb to be as though to be
were all assumption, were willed; and of course it is
and anyone fooled is fooled. Do as you will.
It doesn't matter. What happens to us is not
what happens. It isn't by us. We feel it there.
Listen. Something is living. It is not we.
Aren't we that Adam, still, from whom we are?
The garden is here. I have no way to eat,
have never eaten. I round that fruit.
I push against the branches of that tree.

5 August 1968 / 8 June 1971

William Carlos Williams
The Farmers' Daughters: New Directions, 1961
A True Story about People

Bill was upstairs. (I was visiting 9 Ridge Road, 1954.) Floss was explaining his nervousness whenever the phone rang. He thinks it's for him, a patient. Few seem to realize that 70% of his life has been given to his practice.

She was implying, perhaps, that writing occupied only part of the remaining 30%. But life, like death, has a funny way of getting around percentages. And to read these stories, without exception relating, directly or indirectly, to his work as a G.P. in and out of his office (at home) in Rutherford, New Jersey, is to recognize rather that writing of this order is an extension, not an escape or evasion or diminution, of a man's days and nights.

These sketches, ''verbal transcriptions,'' histories, anecdotes, tales, are all instances of one man's remarkable capacity for love. Love of people, foremost, but no less—with enduring respect —a love of human expressiveness, of language, particular speech, its trickiness, vivacity, penetration.

If I had to choose which, of all the pieces, I preferred most, I suppose I'd say: ''Old Doc Rivers,'' for its groping toward understanding, the openness and clarity of its relations, the way the local is a universe and is again itself; ''The Use of Force,'' for all its anthologizing, a beautiful clean thing, prose, direct in its attack, sure in its sense of when to leave off, its language crisp and true, touching; and ''The Farmers' Daughters,'' perhaps the most ambitious work, with its broken chronology, weaving incident and anecdote, perception and experience, with honest feeling, words falling for words, free and fluent and with complete control.

In some of the earliest pieces I have gritted my teeth at the too heavy sense of the "dialect." The writer seems too much "outside" and making a thing up, not wholly with it, more an idea of something, *not* recounting it, trying too hard to impress. The commitment uncertain, off. But with "Mind and Body" the inside opens:

> . . . I know people think I am a nut. I was an epilep-
> tic as a child. I know I am a manic depressive. But
> doctors are mostly fools. . . .

(I begin to hear the voice of a "later" poet, Robert Creeley, foreshadowed.)

How often, as here, the good doctor tries to project a woman's sense of things, her involvement in/as body, person, place, in things and in "relations." "It is life, what we see and decide for ourselves, that counts."

For response to and a gathering-up of language, in the same story, consider this:

> . . . When I was talking to the Jesuit, who came to
> teach me what the church meant, I told him I could
> not believe that. He said, I should. I asked him, Do
> you? But he did not answer me. . . .

Set it against Charles Olson's "Pastoral Letter," in his *Maximus Poems,* if you want to see evidence of what Dr. Williams has quietly effected "in the art":

> . . . "I don't believe
> I know your name." Given.
> How do you do,
> how do you do. And then:
> "Pardon me, but
> what church
> do you belong to,
> may I ask?"
> . . . .
> I sd, you may, sir.
> He sd, what, sir.
> I sd, none,
> sir. . . .

121

The short, punched-out speech, sporadic, laconic, easy, but not facile, straight-on. Not exaggerated, for the true is crazy enough and hard enough to hang on to, see to, into. And as he gradually works his way out, into the open, he is what he is, William Carlos Williams, half Spanish, half English, part Jewish, part this and part that, man and woman, Pater-son, make no mistake, "Doc," and his wife is Floss, and there are the two boys, and there is the neighborhood. And Rutherford-Paterson opens to contain and be contained to brimming. As a flower in fertile soil. Red roses or "white weeds." Jonquils that "want affection," lore, and raspberries, as one learns, to be picked from a roadside and brought "home" to share.

But is it "art"? The question *is* asked, in and out of school. Sadly. For to express relation with feeling this cleanly, this precisely, without any phoney theatricalism, without resorting to a pompous rhetoric, or a desire to overwhelm with literary machinery, if art is anything, is what this is. There is a glory in people, his glory (as well as ours), the stuff they are made of, we are, stubbornness, indomitability, even within, or particularly within, the confines of ignorance, stupidity, poverty. "He was liked," would be the simplest comment one would expect his townsfolk to say, if asked about him. How could he not be? Concerned about payment, on a visit at whatever hour, but not overly concerned, willing to do it for "nothing," for a laugh or a lark sometimes, for a word or a gesture, a look, for the love of it, for the love of them. For the Polish mother who smiled when she lost her "first daughter" at birth, for the Italian peasant who paid him in snuff. For the love of Mike, sentimental! And yet—how, if the feeling is accurate? He is guilty and proud, moved and obdurate, sensible and sensitive. "I have found . . . that we must live for others, that we are not alone in the world and we cannot live alone."

". . . What was he going to do? How did he know? Where was he going to stay when it got cold? Whose the hell's business was that? What would he eat? Beans and bananas, chewing gum, caviar and roast duck. With that she left him. And later on it grew cold. . . ." A love for the weak and the strong, respect for the offbeat, for the independent soul, for dignity, for sheer cussedness and spite, for a thin body holding out for life, for candor, for generosity, for care. And with a care for the life in language that reveals how American usage (nothing in English prose or poetry

122

contemporary with this work has equal validity) provides leverage for a fresh literature.

But do these stories get "under"? Does anything that is not there? The majority of these recountings, if not all of them, strike me as probably having been written "at the moment," at the spur, or sketched out at once; they are so close to event. Yet, as often as not, there is a "history" involved and I see that much more goes on here than meets the eye: a world, inside. The cadences of speech, the speed and the relaxation, the deftness and alertness of ear and mind, bespeak authority.

In "Old Doc Rivers" he can attack and defend at the same time, and he mutes verdicts:

> Well, Mary, what is it?
> I have a pain in my side, doctor.
> How long have you had it, Mary?
> Today, doctor. It's the first time.
> Just today.
> Yes, doctor.
> Climb up on the table. Pull up your dress.
> Throw that sheet over you. Come on, come on. Up
> with you. Come on now, Mary. Pull up your knees.
> Oooh!
> He could be cruel and crude. And like all who
> are so, he could be sentimentally tender also, and
> painstaking without measure. . . .

As against practitioners of the "tough guy" school, like Hemingway, say, his language is immediately more convincing and accurate, and out of the body, out of the mouth, less manufactured, less "literary." And yet not at all unaware of the problems of what goes, what sticks. He had written, as early as 1932, answering academicism and snobbery:

> . . . I cannot swallow the half-alive poetry which
> knows nothing of totality. . . . Nothing is beyond
> poetry. It is the one solid element on which our lives
> can rely, the "word" of so many disguises, includ-
> ing as it does man's full consciousness, high and
> low, in living objectivity. . . . It is, in its rare major

123

form, a world in fact come to arrest of self realization: that eternity of the present which most stumble over in seeking—or drug themselves into littleness to attain. . . .

The vision, no matter the structure of prose, is a poet's, making poets of us too. Each relation relates one to another. I think any reader will find a coherence; they are "all of a piece." And the "form"? The living speech of a time, a place, a people. All society comes to his feast: children, adults, old folk, animals, Polacks, Wops, Jews, the Irish and Scotch and English, the southerner, the negro (Ralph Ellison confesses to being still a "nigro"), lady and bum, the wise-guy and the tease, the professional and the conversationalist. William Carlos Williams. It sounds already like a crowd. It may be that I recognize a world my own and so feel "at home" and drawn to it. But there's also "more."

It has to do with a man's zest, his brio, his appetite for life, his disgust, or the confrontation of death, an eagerness for and insight into detail, a nose, an ear, an unfailing willingness, desire, to know and know more, to meet "them." He doesnt blink at what he sees either. On the contrary, what he sees makes him want to see more, limitless curiosity, involvement, to speak to a "patient" always as a person, this person and no other, unique in his regard. He makes me want to address my world, wherever I touch it, with equal frankness and affection. Unblinking. Perceiving.

"Down to earth," I'd say. American archaeology, as a friend where I now am staying might put it. Not the classical bit of fancy goods and dream-boats, but the bones, the beads, the chipping stones, flints, arrowheads, artifacts of a difficult and often bare existence, a raw country building. Silver-dollars on a skeleton's eye-sockets. Money plastered everywhere. Seen. Faced. Not pandered to or for. A knowledge, I'd say, that the most beautiful vases are also made of clay. He shapes the pot and paints it with earth's colors.

And no slouch is he as a weaver, out of the so-called "common" thread—to show us, we onlookers, how uncommon our lives may be and often are, as in "The Farmers' Daughters," where he moderates lovingly between two women he knew professionally and as friends, throughout a long career, the very

124

image of his career, the poetry of their lives touching his, or his touch/feeling lifting them into a world of poetry, a world where what is true shines.

His order is that of disorder, but sensed, grasped, embraced, danced with, released. Let be. He says it himself, as of a house of an admired patient:

> . . . I have seldom seen such disorder and brokenness
> —such a mass of unrelated parts of things lying about
> about. That's it! I concluded to myself. An unrecog-
> nizable order! Actually—the new! And so good-
> natured and calm. So definitely the thing! And so
> compact. Excellent. And with such patina of use.
> Everything definitely "painty." . . .

"I'm struck by his honesty and concern, the openness of both."

These are love-stories, all, and one of the quietest of them, "Country Rain," speaks for both himself and Floss of their relation and our relation to them, to others. It opens towards the request for it ("commissioned" by the heart):

> If this were Switzerland, I thought, we'd call it
> lovely: wisps of low cloud rising slowly among the
> heavily wooded hills. But since it's America we call
> it simply wet. Wet and someone at another of the
> tables asks if it's going to stop raining or keep it up
> all day. . . .

To write as simply and fluently and perceptively as that may suggest to some that it's "easy." Don't you believe it. It takes years of listening, of speaking well, of caring to. It requires the mind of a poet.

Perhaps this is more obvious, or will be, in this quote from the end of the same piece. He and Floss, on a wet summer morning gone to pick up the mail for the country house where they are vacationing, find they have "time" and drive on into the old landscape, discussing some of the people they have recently met.

> I stopped the car in a dark, heavily wooded portion
> of the road dripping with the rain from the overhang-
> ing spruces. Floss looked at me. There was a sharp
> drop to the left beyond the half-rotten section of a

125

crude guard rail where in the intense silence a small stream could be heard talking to itself among the stones.

What are you stopping here for?

I want to look at a rock. As I spoke I backed the car about twenty feet, drew in toward the embankment and shut off the engine.

The rock lay at about eye level close to my side of the road, the upper surface of it sloping slightly toward me with the hillside. Not a very big rock. What had stopped me was the shaggy covering which completely inundated it. The ferns, a cropped-short, dark-green fern, was the outstanding feature, growing thickly over an underlying cover of dense moss. But there was also a broad-leafed vine running slightly among the ferns, weaving the pattern together.

That wasn't all. The back portion of the rock, which wasn't much larger than the top of an ordinary dining-room table slightly raised at one side and a little tilted, supported both the rotten stump of a tree long since decayed but, also, a brother to that tree— coming in fact from the same root and very much alive, as big as a man's arm, a good solid arm—a ten-foot tree about whose base a small thicket of brambles clustered. Ferns of three sorts closed in from the sides completing the picture. A most ungrammatical rock.

Isn't this magnificent! Let's bring the two school teachers out here for a ride tomorrow, said Floss. They'd love it. Have you ever talked to them? she added. They're sweet.

No, I said, observing the woods ascending the hillside in the rain. but their situation among the dones, the aints and the seens amuses me. I've been wondering what they are thinking.

Don't worry, said Floss. They know what it's all about.

Look, I said, after we had rolled forward another half mile or so, do you see what I see?

Oh, said Floss, raspberries!

We stopped again. It was still raining, so I told her to stay where she was while I got down to pick some of the fruit, the remainder of what I could see had been an abundant crop recently growing at the side of the road sloping toward the stream.

Oh, taste them! said Flossie when I had brought them to her in my hand. They're dripping with juice. Anyone who would put sugar on such berries, well, would be just a barbarian. Perhaps we could stop again here tomorrow and pick enough for everybody.

A steady, heavy rain, she added. The farmers will like that. And then as an afterthought: Do you think Ruth will ever marry?

Why? I answered her.

I'd be a barbarian to add more. But I can't refrain from this from the beginning of the next story "Inquest" and let that be it:

What we save, what we have, what we do. No matter. That which we most dearly cherish, *that* we shall lose, the one thing we most desire. What remains?

To be and remain interesting—with reservations —perhaps. . . .

Stories? Yes: "a world in fact come."

(from *The Massachusetts Review*, Winter 1962)

At: *Bottom*

I cannot "read" music. It's fair enough to fancy that most other
interested parties will be equally abysmally ignorant, though I'd
not boast of the fact, nor suggest a need of sympathy. On the
contrary, I suggest only what everything else in these two volumes
bound in one case (*casa?*) suggests: see with minding eyes what
the heart presents as issue.

Ze-ami said, in relation to his theatre:

> There are two ways of conceiving the song:
> either the author of the libretto, knowing music,
> composes a flowing harmonious text, or the singer,
> setting the text to music, scores the articulation.
>
> Forget the voice, get to the modulations; forget
> the modulations, get to the tones; forget the tones,
> feel the rhythms.
>
> When, after years of practise and experience,
> song becomes the way in which one presents oneself
> to the world, the dance is song, and one is a master,
> all elements according to each engaged.

Apart from my ignorance, then, there is what is there that
anyone can see who has the eyes that care to, and that I have

---

*Bottom: On Shakespeare, by Louis Zukofsky, and *Shakespeare's Pericles* set
to music by Celia Zukofsky, published in two volumes, boxed, by the Ark
Press for The Humanities Research Center, The University of Texas, 1963.

found available. The music, needing no criticism from me, sounds the sounds that the words make on the page as they fall together. The notations are gracefully simple. I may not know what a cluster of notes sliding down a slope may sound like, but I know what they "feel" like in relation to the words they work to. And I cannot, or maybe dont want to, imagine any poet, young or old, not being interested in so clear a music to so dear a text.

After all, what is any book dealing with anyone's poems about? If it doesnt bring one closer to the poetry, make one want and know more ardently that intimacy poetry provides with what life most is, then something that could be done has not been, something is "rotten." And here we are not simply "led on" by the words of Volume One, but to the table and the nourishment we need to go on with, the love, without more ado.

The words assist. To repeat, in another way, what any work we know as art attempts is to project man's devotion to life, such as it is, in whatever way "takes"; i.e., in such a way that the insistence of moment remains to heighten it, so that a man may say: I *am* alive, and *feel* it, and *care* to feel it, to go on, not merely *from* that point but *at* it.

Take a coin, say, and place it in the palm of your hand. You see it and soon have evaluated it. At first there is a sense of weight and contact (timbre), eyes have gathered shape and design and color-light, but quite soon there is no weight, except the dead weight of the hand held up, and the eye is long since bored. One feels a fool for bothering. But the work of art, which could conceivably be a coin, is just such coin as retains its weight or alters it surprisingly as every look discovers new wealth and worth, and the hand held up suddenly makes sense. As if a prayer were answered in the praying hands. Or, indeed, one doesnt have to think *about* it: the experience proves event. So beauty is precisely what keeps bringing home to us our own weight, with due proportion (the world within and without), the only balance that *will* keep.

Not since Coleridge has any poet attempted to such an extent to bring to weight the complete work of Shakespeare as Zukofsky has here. It answers, far more cogently than any argument, also for the relation that obtains between the English language as it is handled now anywhere and as it has been, anywhere. Poetry alone, language brought to fruition, has this bearing for us. So that the accomplishment here serves as measure for all poetry, past present and future, that cares for itself emphasizing the one theme that binds the work and brings us close:

> Things base and vile, holding no quantity,
> Love can transpose to form and dignity.
> Love looks not with the eyes but with the mind.

Coleridge, inveigled by the pursuit of Schelling, tended to textual interpretation and psychological nuance. His own mind also, of course, had long since lost its way with poetry. Zukofsky keeps to the heart of the texts, adding only those of his own and others he has probed that merit concordance and find it. To give a sense of what he comes to I can only sketch, through some key quotes, evidences and as response of my own add notes to bear that sense further out.

1

After the brief preface, to which I've already alluded in my own above, Zukofsky, upon introducing Bottom in apology for saying ''more'' about Shakespeare, risks his ears as he employs his mind's eyes. The first brief section, an emendation of the basic theme, brings on one of the major figures of the book, Baruch Spinoza, whose intellect so beautifully extends out of and into the Works of Shakespeare—as though Spinoza were Shakespeare's first fine reader and commentator. Comes a study of Shakespeare's intention and achievement, without either scraping or heaping up, in a series of personal statements and quotations that reach fullest pitch in ''The Phoenix and the Turtle,'' which sounds the remainder of the book and these pages.

To begin: Zukofsky finds Jonson's answer to his own celebrated lament of Shakespeare's unblotted lines worth quoting and then himself comments for all our sakes:

> . . . Jonson's lines convey the contest any poet has
> with his art: working towards a perception that is his
> mind's peace, he knows, unfortunately, that his writ-
> ing with fleshly pencils will be loosely considered the
> issue of himself.

130

And it is also overlooked that Shakespeare must have, duty-bound to his theatre, as actor and shareholder, as well as writer and likely "director," composed much of his work "live," literally on the stage, with the actors' voices particular in his ears, their gait and girth a very part of his sense of history's possibility as "drama."

Zukofsky mildly but firmly addresses the scholar critics:

> Guessing at the chronology of the forty-four items of the canon, the critics have been insistent on seeing his ideas grow, his feelings mature, his heart go through more exploits than a heart can, except as may be vaguely intimated from the beat and duration of any of the lines or works. It is simpler to consider the forty-four items of the canon as one work, sometimes poor, sometimes good, sometimes great, always regardless of time in which it was composed, and so, despite defects of quality, durable as one thing from "itself never turning." So growth is organic to decay and vice versa.

And Zukofsky, that most honorable expositor of love in our time, at once appends:

> Love, or . . . the desire to project the mind's peace, is one growth.

Or as he has Shakespeare to source him: "Love's not Time's fool, etc."

Definitions of love naturally accrue, from the Works. Into Spinoza:

> . . . It is necessary that we should not be released from love, because on account of the frailty of our nature we should not be able to exist without having something to enjoy with which we might be united and strengthened.

And back to:

> Love looks not with the eyes but with the mind.

and more comment:

. . . the definition is one with the craft displayed by the action of the writing. . . . The words show their task: a pursuit of elements and proportions necessary for invention that, like love as discerned object, is empowered to act on the intellect.

And the turn is toward the nature of how words work:

. . . The tendency . . . is for the sound to persist as pun or tenuous intellectual echo, unless these words are spoken over and over again, or, what amounts to the same process, unless the actual print preserves them for the eye to fathom but not to see. . . . "When icicles hang by the wall." It takes a competent musician to suspect their musical melody.

And he sees that

The best in the writing called *The Tempest* resembles, after all, the corporeality of Ariel's songs, not what finally happens to Ariel when his freedom becomes as insubstantial as Love's asking, tragic, fractious "mind."

Zukofsky has a way of sounding his reader. Our flaws tell something of how the clay was wrought and how the firing may sometimes misfire and fail to ring true, because of it. He says, turning the trope:

Each play rings tunes on all the others. And the *Works* say one thing: love, the seed of the writing that reveals nothing of Shakespeare but his text, moves all the leaves of his book to sound different degrees of "Love's mind" or its relative failures of judgment. For, by definition, only love looking with the eyes has perfect taste.

And he shapes, as the wheel spins, a simple but essential statement of what theatre is for language when he writes:

The form of all uttered drama must arise from the measured order of words moving to a visual end.
"Arise arise. . . ."

When you realize, abruptly, that so far I have taken this much

132

space to discuss Zukofsky's text of 470 pages and have done only the first 19, you get some notion of how concentrated and constellated an experience the words he conjures up is.

He sees, as few seem to have seen, that *Hamlet* is the tragedy of love's innocence brought to terrible wisdom and the dignity that hollows out justice from it: "The *tragic* theme," as he says, "of love's division from reason because it cannot see and 'will not know what all but he do know.' "

Zukofsky ranges "freely" through the field of the *Works* to find his and Shakespeare's theme "discovered," finding it even in mere prosody, confounding editors who think in terms of unblinking perfection.

It comes to "The Phoenix and the Turtle" reverberatingly:

> Reason, in itself confounded,
> Saw division grow together,
> To themselves yet either neither,
> Simple were so well compounded;
>
> That it cried, How true a twain
> Seemeth this concordant one!
> Love hath reason, reason none,
> If what parts can so remain.

And Zukofsky leaves Spinoza's words to sound Shakespeare's out:

> . . . the mind no less feels those things which it conceives in understanding than those which it has in memory. For the eyes of the mind by which it sees things and observes them are proofs.

Nor is it irrelevant here to close upon Joyce's transformation of Aquinas (partly alluded to later in *Bottom*, p. 214, when *Ulysses* enters) in *Stephen Hero*, since it has the feel of this selfsame conjunction:

> (Stephen discusses "relentlessly" his exploration of esthetic theory with Cranly)
> . . . The apprehensive faculty must be scrutinized in action.
> —Yes. . . .
> —You know what Aquinas says: The three things requisite for beauty are, integrity, a wholeness,

symmetry and radiance. Some day I will expand that sentence into a treatise. Consider the performance of your own mind when confronted by any object, hypothetically beautiful. Your mind to apprehend that object divides the entire universe into two parts, the object, and the void which is not the object. To apprehend it you must lift it away from everything else: and then you perceive that it is one integral thing, that is *a* thing. You recognise its integrity. Isn't that so?

—And then?

—That is the first quality of beauty: it is declared in a simple sudden synthesis of the faculty which apprehends. What then? Analysis then. The mind considers the object in whole and in part, in relation to itself and to other objects, examines the balance of its parts, contemplates the form of the object, traverses every cranny of the structure. So the mind receives the impression of the symmetry of the object. The mind recognises that the object is in the strict sense of the word, a *thing,* a definitely constituted entity. You see?

—Let us turn back, said Cranly.

. . . but Stephen took his arm summarily and led him away.

—Now for the third quality. For a long time I couldn't make out what Aquinas meant. He uses a figurative word (a very unusual thing for him) but I have solved it. *Claritas* is *quidditas.* After the analysis which discovers the second quality the mind makes the only logically possible synthesis and discovers the third quality. This is the moment which I call epiphany. First we recognise that the object is *one* integral thing, then we recognise that it is an organised composite structure, a *thing* in fact: finally, when the relation of the parts is exquisite, when the parts are adjusted to the special point, we recognise that it is *that* thing which it is. Its soul, its whatness, leaps to us from the vestment of its appearance. The soul of the commonest object, the structure of which is so

134

adjusted, seems to us radiant. The object achieves its ephiphany.

Or as Horatio saw fit to report to Hamlet of a father's ghost:

> . . . as they had delivered, both in time,
> Form of the thing, each word made true and good,
> The apparition comes. . . .

2

Part Two is entitled: *"Music's master:* notes for Her music to *Pericles* and for a graph of culture.'' It is itself in two parts, the first only a handful of pages, the second bringing one to page 94 and the Alphabet of Subjects, which runs the remainder of the book, apart from the helpful Index.

The brief section opening Part Two works out of the exact use of eyes in Shakespeare, using an alphabetical image of Shakespeare, proving he may have written his words "in air," but saw in any event each letter also for what it was worth as an active component of the goings-on:

> *Scarus:* I had a wound here that was like a T,
> But now 'tis made an H.
> (*Antony and Cleopatra,* IV, vii, 8)

It is this "H" that has activated Zukofsky's capital letter in the section's heading, "Her music." It is a marriage of true minds, no matter how eccentric it may at first appear, for Z. has perceived the capital to lead to music of *Pericles,* not as a staged character but as a text which assumes the shape of music. 'Tis an ingenuity whose "scope" he says "appraises a refinement of eyes into mind, *affined* (in the sense, of which Shakespeare is said to have used the word, of being *bound by obligation*) to judgment as a phase of taste, when the sense of the tongue is changed into a draught and a morsel of thought." But I havent the heart to quote what then follows of his reading of "H," for any poet would want that heave entirely for himself.

I'd add to what he says, touching the sentence of Scarus, that Shakespeare sees even more than the shape of letters, the dramatic occasion in them. For one is not expected to look sideways to get

135

that H from that T, but to see the T, as a body, fallen on *its* side (wise), with the addition of a stroke. It's what ''eyes'' a man who lives theatre could come up with. How much, indeed, of Shakespeare sees this well, draws from such economy and store and often at most crucial moment.

In the longer concluding segment of Part Two Zukofsky extends the purview of his book in time, from Aristotle to Wittgenstein, retaining the instances of Spinoza as pivot, finding in all their work Shakespeare's projections focussed *as* thought, and creating a nexus of man's capacity eloquently attested to. Whether the ability and the care to make so magnificent an ''integration'' of ''minds'' and ''eyes'' and ''love'' occurs in art elsewhere today so extensively remains a task to see. In any event, this (*Bottom*) is an opportunity that has called only in our time and only an intelligence equally aware of the rest of the world's achievements could amend fully what is given here. (And it is a sign of Zukofsky's clairvoyant love that it sees *that* possibility and intimates as much.)

Zukofsky also sees that Shakespeare knows

> No tongue! all eyes! Be silent

which discovers answer in Paulina's words to Leontes:

> Behold, and say 'tis well.
> I like your silence, it the more shows off
> Your wonder: but yet speak. . . .

But now the proportion:

> *love : reason :: eyes : mind*

perpends. And the author explains: ''Love needs no tongue of reason if love and eyes are *1*—an identity. The good reasons of the mind's right judgment are but superfluities for saying: *Love sees*—if it needs saying at all in a text which is always hovering towards *The rest is silence*.''

> (An *aside:* For some reason which misses me—but I have always proven a poor target for reasons—Zukofsky's very care, which only comes alive to equal care, *will* be abused as being too difficult or obscure. I can think of no poet who has every been at greater

136

pains to be clear and simple "enough" *and* to be as patient in explaining his "meanings." *Bottom* is, if anything, the very touchstone of such patience. Sometimes, honestly, I wish he were *less* gentle with his reader. But courtesy is his character and grace his instinct, as poetry his mode.)

The rest of Part Two is a counterpoint of texts, husbanded to point conjunctions with the theme perpended (Shakespeare's words interposed throughout to keep encounter clear): Aristotle, Spinoza, Wittgenstein and a few apropos passages from Boole.

One example may suffice of the exquisitely "fitted" exposition that largely says itself. Wittgenstein's *Tractatus:*

4.022: The proposition *shows* its sense. The proposition *shows* how things stand, *if* it is true. And it *says* that they do so stand.

The author remarks:

Shakespeare's text is always thinking of such propositions, flying from and returning to them. So Launce (in *Two Gentlemen of Verona*), Chaplinesque, visibly endeared to other bodies by the respects in which they agree, while his voice distills indiscriminably from feeling, sense, as Aristotle might say, the adequate ideas granted common to all men.

Launce. Marry, after they clos'd in earnest, they parted very fairly in jest.

Speed. But shall she marry him?

Launce. No.

Speed. How then? Shall he marry her?

Launce. No, neither.

Speed. What, are they broken?

Launce. No, they are both as whole as a fish.

Speed. Why, then, how stands the matter with them?

Launce. Marry, thus: when it stands well with him, it stands well with her.

Speed. What an ass art thou! I understand thee not.

Launce. What a block art thou, that thou canst not! My staff understands me.

Speed. What thou say'st?

Launce. Ay, and what I do too. Look thee, I'll but
lean, and my staff understands me.

Speed. It stands under thee indeed.

Launce. Why, stand-under and under-stand is all one.

And the next proposition of the *Tractatus* drops:

4.023: The proposition determines reality to this
extent, that one only needs to say ''yes'' or ''no''
to make it agree with reality.

This reminds me of a Vedantic anecdote Zimmer relates in his
Philosophies of India:

The king of the present story, who became a pupil of
the philosopher Shankara (9th century A.D.), was a
man of sound and realistic mind who could not get
over the fact of his own royal splendor and august
personality. When his teacher directed him to regard
all things, including the exercise of power and enjoy-
ment of kingly pleasure, as no more than equally
indifferent reflexes (purely phenomenal) of the tran-
scendental essence that was the Atman not only of
himself but of all things, he felt some resistance. And
when he was told that that one and only Atman was
made to seem multiple by the deluding-force of his
own inborn ignorance, he determined to put his guru
to the test and prove whether he would behave as a
person absolutely unconcerned.

The following day, therefore, when the philosopher was coming along one of the stately approaches to the palace, to deliver his next lecture to the
king, a large and dangerous elephant, maddened by
heat, was let loose at him. Shankara turned and fled
the moment he perceived his danger, and when the
animal nearly reached his heels, disappeared from
view. When he was found, he was at the top of a lofty
palm tree, which he had ascended with a dexterity
more usual among sailors than intellectuals. The elephant was caught, fettered, and conducted back to
the stables, and the great Shankara, perspiration
breaking from every pore, came before his pupil.

138

Politely, the king apologized to the master of cryptic wisdom for the unfortunate, nearly disastrous incident; then, with a smile scarcely concealed and half pretending great seriousness, he inquired why the venerable teacher had resorted to physical flight, since he must have been aware that the elephant was of a purely illusory, phenomenal character.

The sage replied, "Indeed, in highest truth, the elephant is non-real. Nevertheless, you and I are as non-real as that elephant. Only your ignorance, clouding the truth with this spectacle of non-real phenomenality, made you see phenomenal me go up a non-real tree."

Or Zukofsky:

In answering that fancy is bred in the eyes Shakespeare's song ("Tell me where is fancy bred, / Or in the heart or in the head?") bypasses two of the most familiar certainties of all thoughtful certain nature. The question and the cadence may suggest that the heart beats and the head counts. The reply relies "simply" on the eye—Aristotle's lighting, self-delighting and beloved eye that looks to know or, even when harnessed for intellectual action, also takes pleasure in seeing—the purest organ of sense. And if love—or action of desire, imagination, and intellect—must die in the eyes that engender it, the song is no sadder for the knell of its refrain. It is as Aristotle's eye had it having seen white: *it will not be good any the more for being eternal, since that which lasts long is no whiter than that which perishes in a day.*

> (Recurring in *"A"-12* as:
> Nothing is better for being eternal
> Or more white than white that dies
> of a day.)

Or as *The Winter's Tale* tells it as the living statue is revealed and Paulina says:

> ... If I thought the sight of my poor image
> Would thus have wrought you (for the stone is mine)
> I'd not have showed it.
> ... No longer shall you gaze on't, lest your fancy
> May think anon, it moves. ...

And Leontes, teased, can only cry out:

> No settled sense of the World can match
> The pleasure of that madness. ...

It is, as Zukofsky notices:

> Shakespeare's *Works* as they conceive history regret
> a great loss of physical looking. They recall with the
> abstracted "look" of a late time. ... [They] say:
> seeing should be the object of speech (which in fabl-
> ing time resolves into song), rather than that speech
> ... should be the object of seeing.

> "Daruma
> *found object*
> that is art. ...."

And leads to an evaluation of Shakespeare's work and any poet's, as the section pulls to its curtain, "... that is, the feeling that his writing as a whole world *is,* compelling any logic o philosophy of history not to confuse an expression of *how it is* with *that world is.* The thought that *it is* has, of course, no value, is rather of a region where thought is free and music is for nothing—or as eyes see and go out. The value of the thought *how it is* is that it is against confusing expression. In this sense the preference for eyes he finds in Shakespeare may caution him [the reader] not to plot his graph of culture too hurriedly as he thinks about the implications of the preference imputed to Shakespeare. The constant of Shakespeare's expression—whether the words say *All eyes!* or *I want no eyes; I stumbled when I saw*—or what any reader sees, hears, or thinks into them—is (for the purpose of asserting the sense of positive and negative propositions) its inexpressible *trust of expression*, the incentive and end of which is to unite others to it in friendship."

140

Because there is so much and so much must be attempted in such an effort as *Bottom* Zukofsky not wishing "to draw an end to thinking but merely to show its limits" leads us, "speaking as must happen, trusting to see an alphabet of subjects." This is then, in Part Three, which fulfils the book, his spelling out of what there is of Shakespeare's theme of "love's eyes" in an alphabetical treatment of what occurs to it to him. His "A" here, which only grazes that larger treat of his own of that title, as well as its prefiguring in "Thanks to the Dictionary" (in *It Was*), continuing his life into ours, is AS ARISTOTLE ARTICULATED TO THE FIRST FISHERMAN "The implicit alchemy in the atomic table of the human animal." Bombs away. And he can say amidst his bit on the first letter of our ignorance, amidst Wittgenstein's propositions and gradually Shakespeare, "The examples of explosive processes that are necessary if conceived as goods or ends fasten precisely on the meaning of *final cause.* It is the order and form of the snake, tail in its mouth; or of the colorful flower that eats insects—to which thought may say 'yes' or 'no.' Otherwise life is nothing, thought is nothing . . . replacing the word *sphere* by *fear* . . . is a matter of saying 'no' where Aristotle originally said 'yes' " and Shakespeare, as Z sees, says:

> What I have been I have forgot to know. . . .
> For that I am a man, pray see me buried.

Rainer Maria Rilke in a letter of 1923 can add to this this:

> . . . I reproach all modern religions for having handed to their believers consolations and glossings over of death, instead of administering to them the means of reconciling themselves to it and coming to an understanding with it. With it, with its full, unmasked cruelty: this cruelty is so tremendous that it is just with it that the circle closes: it leads right back again into the extreme of a mildness that is great, pure and perfectly clear (all consolation is turbid) as we have never surmised mildness to be, not even on the sweetest spring day. But toward the experiencing of this most profound mildness which, were only a few of us to feel it with conviction, could perhaps little

by little penetrate and make *transparent* all the relations of life: toward the experiencing of *this* most rich and most sound mildness, mankind has never taken even the first steps—unless in its oldest, most innocent times, whose secret has been all but lost to us. The content of "initiations" was, I am sure, nothing but the imparting of a "key" that permitted the reading of the word "death" *without* negation; like the moon, life surely has a side permanently turned away from us which is not its counter-part but its complement toward perfection, toward consummation, toward the truly sound and full sphere and orb of being.

One should not fear that our strength might not suffice to bear any experience of death, even were it the nearest and the most terrible; death is not beyond our strength; it is the measure mark at the vessel's rim: we are *full* as often as we reach it—and being full means (for us) being heavy . . . that is all. —I will not say that one should *love* death; but one should love life so magnanimously, so without calculation and selection that spontaneously one constantly includes with it and loves death too (life's averted half)—which is in fact what happens also, irresistibly and illimitably, in all great impulses of love! Only because we exclude death in a sudden moment of reflection, has it turned more and more into something alien, and as we have kept it in the alien, something hostile. . . .

Under "Birthplace" Zukofsky recalls for Shakespeare, for us, that "eyes involve a void; eyes also avoid the abstruse beyond their focus" and that Shakespeare's "I's," his Clotens and Calibans, no less, see that *"love should see* flows around their words and shows them all the more their sightless tune which does not find its rests so as to draw breath or sequence."

Here we are with Henry James at Stratford-on-Avon "doing" the place and finding the capital H breathing more uprightly on us again:

". . . It's rather a pity you know, that He isn't here.
I mean as Goethe's at Weimar. For Goethe *is* at Weimar."

"Yes, my dear; that's Goethe's bad luck. There
he sticks. *This* man isn't anywhere. I defy you to
catch Him. . . ."

Or H.J. to Lubbock:

> . . . the portent of that brilliance, that prodigality
> . . . emerging out of what?—out of nothing, out of
> darkness, out of the thick provincial mind; from
> which a figure steps forth, a young man of ill condi-
> tion, a lout from Stratford, this *lout. . . .*

C is "Continents." The exploratory mind. And how those
who were entrusted his work, Shakespeare's territory, introduced
him to us, Misters Heminge and Condell, who could say and make
us see they knew:

> [These plays] . . . are now offer'*d* to your view cur'*d*
> and *perfect of their limbes;* and all the rest, absolute
> in their numbers, as he conceived them *Who, as he
> was a happie imitator of Nature, was a most gentle
> expresser of it. His mind and hand went together* . . .
> we hope, to your divers capacities, you will find
> enough, both to draw, *and to hold you:* for his wit
> *can no more lie hid,* then it could be lost. Reade
> him, therefore; and againe, and againe: And if then
> you doe not like him, surely you are in some *mani-
> fest danger, not to understand him.* And so we leave
> you to other of his Friends, whom if you need, can
> bee your guides: if you neede them not, you can
> leade your selves, and others. And such Readers we
> *wish* him.

The eyes here are large, beyond any prejudice but love's, at
that depth, which is bottom, and see that "Asia, Africa, and
Europe offered the knowledge and sight that fed Shakespeare's
thought of eyes." Or as Zukofsky sees, and Zimmer sees, that in
the "old" tongues the words of deepest meaning adhere still to the
things of the world, never go dull-abstract and merely "philosophical." Of Indian thought Zimmer says, in terms of its language:

The nouns, for example, which constitute the bulk
of the philosophic terminology, stand side by side
with verbs that have been derived from the same
roots and denote activities or processes expressive of
the same content. One can always come to the basic
meaning through a study of the common uses of the
word in daily life. . . .

Zukofsky, who doesnt have to read *everything,* seeing as he
reads what he does, reports from his ground:

In Hebrew the word for *word* is also the word for
thing. The roots and stems of grammar are foresights
and hindsights so entangled that traditions and chro-
nologies mean little if not an acceptance, a love of
certain, living beings for words as seen things.

Strange as it may appear the relation of one discovering the
weights and measures, the sounds and soundings of what to him,
one hopes, will always be a "strange new" language, is found in
this sentence a student recently in Osaka engineered about a bird,
mining the "i's" for sound, if not minding the eyes for grammar's
rules:

White eyes are easy to take to men, so was mine, but
it flied away unexpectedly.

Shakespeare's eyes, bless them as they bless us, could compass the startling simplicity and rightness (*not* righteousness) of:

Glory is like a circle in the water.

And it is as clear a statement, say, as the recognition in Vico of
how the mind's eye extends:

We demonstrate mathematics, because we create its
truth.

Or Han-shan, who perhaps saw further from his perch,
saying:

Forget going
Let direction speak.

But Zukofsky clarifies in this largest section what he is about:

All weighing here under *Continents* leads nowhere
or to this: the Cabalist Isaac ben Abraham ben David
of Posquières in Provence was called *Sagi-nahor,
very clear-sighted,* a euphemism—a Jew's jest for
blind; yet the sensible subject of Cabbalah was the
visible creation, no matter how the Letters group,
emanate, go secret.

Shakespeare read—

It is absurd to say and expound what he read.
Could he not have heard at second hand, seeing? . . .

In these circumstances one can imagine an
anthology of things Shakespeare's lines—as eyes so
to speak—would like to have read—much as Bottom
who never tells his dream thinks "to get Peter
Quince to write a ballad of this dream."

Note how the word "things" assumes Hebraic dimension here (as
words in Zukofsky have a way, weigh, of remembering themselves)
and how his sense of Bottom's comedy completes it with care, or
as he himself has elsewhere put it, within another context of
Aristotle:

When love laughs that carefully it has eyes.

The anthology that proceeds then requires little comment, but
commends itself to each man's experience and, as I feel it would—
and does where the work is concerned—to Shakespeare's, for
which reason it is here.

All I, in turn, can care to do is draw some strand of melody
out here and there from amongst the many quotes, set with such
remarkable lucidity; that is, sounding the eyes of hearts and minds
that see to Shakespeare's tune and, as ancilla, clear such quotations
I have lived that answer to it too, or touch.

Of the Bacon brought home as Shakespeare Zukofsky straight-
way says:

There should be no objection to some such notion as
that Bacon read Shakespeare, or had heard him
speak, or had listened to his lines; or that Shakespeare, fascinated by Bacon's mulling talk, used it as
any poet might with or without obligation.

145

I'd like to believe as well that Bacon might have entered theatres of Shakespeare's performance and found experience there for words to mull.

> There is no proof: *except* that Bacon's antitheses always doubt as much as they confirm "We see it, we see it." But with Shakespeare's lines the tensions of "We see it" invariably compose an insistent form *and* thought *and* action whose seen "truth can never be confirm'd enough, / Though doubts did ever sleep."

Beyond cavil I'd turn to the Chinese *Book of Odes* and what Ezra Pound has seen of what is there:

> As thought delights in water
> by the half-circling pool
> picking pond-weed,
> hooves clicking clearly
> high feet of horses:
> clear his fame, clear his face,
> clear his laugh is, to teach without anger
> in this place.

Zukofsky finding Persia in Emerson finds:

> The privates of man's heart
> They speken and sound in his ear
> As tho' they loud winds were;
> . . . the sense of a half-translated ode of Hafiz. . . . Passion adds eyes—is a magnifying glass. . . . We use resemblances of logic until experience puts us in possession of real logic. . . . In certain hours we can almost pass our hand through our own body. . . . Style betrays . . . as eyes do. . . . That only can we see which we are, and which we make . . . and that for every thought its proper melody or rhyme exists, though the odds are immense against our finding it . . . the best thoughts run into the best words; imaginative and affectionate thoughts, into music. . . .

which leads me to find in Hopkins:

146

My heart, where have we been? What have we seen,
    my mind?

Or more connectedly directly with Shakespeare, or how eyes meet
in words and see through others' *more:*

> *Journal* (1867):
> July 18. Showers and fine; rainbow. —The reason
> Shakspere calls it "the blue bow" (*The Tempest*,
> IV, i, 80)—to put it down now precisely—is because
> the blue band edged by and ending in violet, though
> not the broadest, is the deepest expression of colour
> in the bow and so becomes the most decisive and em-
> phatic feature there.

Nearly a year later GMH notes:

> July 6. Rainy till lately (5 o'clock), when a low rain-
> bow backed by the Black Forest hills, which were
> partly dimmed out with wet mist, appeared, and—
> what I never saw before—rays of shadow crossed it,
> all its round, and where they crossed it paled the
> colour. It was a "blue bow". . . .

Surely this is how love works, sees and helps see. The
moment that strikes with sudden appearance brings to mind, or is
the mind that brings to appearance, such touches of sight that
beloved Shakespeare wrought and wrings in poet's eyes.

The same Hopkins who wrote two settings for Shakespeare's
"Who is Sylvia?" with its: "Beauty lives with kindness. / Love
doth to her eyes repair / to help him of his blindness."

In his *Journal* again (1873):

> May 11—Bluebells in Hodder wood, all hanging
> their heads one way. I caught as well as I could while
> my companions talked the Greek rightness of their
> beauty, the lovely / what people call / "gracious"
> bidding one to another or all one way, the level or
> stage or shire of colour they make hanging in the air
> a foot above the grass, and a notable glare the eye
> may abstract and sever from the blue colour / of light
> beating up from so many glassy heads, which like
> water is good to float their deeper instress in upon
> the mind

147

May 12—"Under the blossom that hangs on the bow": cherry blossoms for instance hang down in tufts and tassels *under* the bough that bears it. . . . Aug. 10.—Some yellow spoons came up with the tumblers after dinner. Somebody said they were brass and I tasted them to find out and it seemed so. Some time afterwards as I came in from a stroll with Mr. Purbrick he told me Hügel had said the scarlet or rose colour of flamingos was found to be due to a fine copper powder on the feathers. As he said this I tasted the brass in my mouth. . . .

Clearly it's impossible to read Hopkins without seeing the sense he could make of what he saw, taste what he tasted, feel what he felt, so beautifully do his words project experience and bring us to it. How words "weigh" is most exquisite here, for Hopkins' drawings, at which he went with a certain avidity too, look, though accurate, hopelessly "tame" and vapid beside these fleshed accuracies.

What a wonder it would be, and poetry, if scientists could write as free of jargon and with as true an eye, as hearted an eye, as this! What a revolution "science" could be as *life!*

Comes an eye for color and Zukofsky through his Shakespeare fastens "green," using eyes too of Thomistic angels. So that he can say: "Phantasms render unquiet *the act* and *a this somewhat* of Shakespeare's intelligible identification of reason with sight, which turns to its object (color). And precisely because *phantasms* are habitual to the *possible intellect* of the Plays, the reason of their lines does not encourage or intend more science or theology than the angels see—than a *now* that stands still. . . ."

> One sense cannot prove
> Another false.
> There are places out of sight
> Filled with voices.
> What the mind sees
> And the eyes see—the
> Shape of their ground, the same.
> (from *"A"-12*)

Or: "in passages of *Advancement in Learning* Francis Bacon, in the manner of Shakespeare's text on things and nations, conveys a sense that takes *heed* to *have open eye''* and knows perhaps experience, seeing through bias. How the theme reaches every which way out of time into it again: not only that Shakespeare did not *not* see always what was his time and place, his day and his night, the whites and the blacks, Shylock and Othello, but every jaundiced quirk of human nature feeds wordwise the appetite and itch for violence. And how it jumps in the very news we read from Birmingham or those who see to it we do:

> It was an old black man in Atlanta who looked into
> my eyes and directed me into my first segregated bus.
> I have spent a long time thinking about that man. I
> never saw him again. [A Zukofskyian dog, no doubt.]
> I cannot describe the look which passed between us,
> as I asked him for directions, but it made me think,
> at once, of Shakespeare's ''the oldest have borne
> most.'' It made me think of the blues: *Now, when a*
> *woman gets the blues, Lord, she hangs her head and*
> *cries. But when a man gets the blues, Lord, he grabs*
> *a train and rides.*
>
> (James Baldwin, *Nobody Knows My Name*)

> . . . And for the rest of the time I was in the South I
> watched the eyes of old black men.

In such eyes, whose experience lies buried within them or their scar-tissue, is the eloquence of such long suffering and the patience no man wants but some achieve.

If you think I digress, you mistake the eyes that never leave off:

> That art is ''good'' which does not presume or run
> out on the world but becomes part of visible, audible,
> or thinkable nature: an art reached with scaled mat-
> ter, when it is, as in Shakespeare with words, in
> Bach with sounds, in Euclid with concepts, or in Ra-
> venna mosaic with small colored stones.

This requires as well a sense of what goes, more than ''passes,'' of integrity:

> . . . structure of no one structure, unsubmissively
> uncomposed, unseen and yet to be seen as a new kind

—as paint that is sculpture like Michelangelo's *Alle-gorical Figure* accomplished under patronage, or arrogance, by an honest man on his back on a scaffolding at the risk of his life, and placed where to be seen is to be forced to see—they are not resigned to palpable humanity that would restrict them to a scale in the extended world.

Considering, too, how eyes in Egyptian statues light on us makes us feel the inward look of rock, how, when spirit reaches rock to find its shape there, light breaks loose. The scribe's eyes look to our eyes to take our words down. The young Amenophis holding the younger Nefertiti's hand, or hers rather overlapping his in common rock, looks in his eyes alive to that contact in ours, with a grace and modesty that makes us mutually tremble. The old cracked wood (blockhead of under-standing?) of the Sheik El-Beled bears in the tilt of his gaze and the stalwart plant of his feet a sturdiness, endurance, confidence, that outfaces us, giving us face. And how much peace in the paired eyes (paradise?) is contributed through the stock of great stone couples quarried from Egyptian temples and tombs to make museums magnificent? We may well be terrified at what power their eyes retain, demand of ours, that ours have largely abandoned to photogravure.

All the more reason to return—to the present—to what sensitive eyes encouraged in speech have garnered for us here, free of glass cases:

> All art after Shakespeare may be read to suffer the
> loss which the excesses of thought and afterthought
> in his lines hide of the simple intention *to be seen.*

How Hamlet, a character in a play, thinks of the actors about to play his play and rants to the point of accusing himself of acting: all to conceal from himself, while revealing himself more deeply to us, that he wants more palpable spur for his still "dull revenge."

> . . . art after him is distracted by the "reason" of his
> lines tho these constantly say: only the love of eyes
> reassures the reasonable.

Zukofsky sees straight as Shakespeare sees straight: the blacks are rich with color, the whites (of eyes) are penetrated, move invisible co-extensive space. Words create a theatre where actors live dance, imagination finds body.

150

. . . in Shakespeare . . . Songs . . speeches . . . are
"natural breath"—art is as plain as Durham Cathedral; beauty, not more out of the way than moss that
greens shape of trunk and stone. This much of Shakespeare exists in contrast to all the advances of art
which are functions of mind. "Perspectives," as
used in the Plays, means illusions; or the represen-
tational equivalent of being not in range and touch;
or an approach to objects with such impetus that the
eye not seeing shape is literally impressed by blurs of
light and shade; by impasto it may momentarily wish
to scrape away to get at the color. . . .
. . . The least reflective lines of Shakespeare are
nearer Oriental painting—before painting that studied plein-air, optics and spectra; are with the order of
art whose feeling works out as the eye moves over
surface—up, down, over, diagonally, across; with
ochre's red and yellow following the natural contour
or bas-relief of animal over cave rock; and if clas-
sifiers term Shakespeare *barocco*, his accomplishment
is not a metaphor for music—a matter of what the
eyes see flowing away in the mind, but of presence
joined by the fixed curve.

Art is to see.

Nor is it "off" to mention here that Shakespeare's stage as
Leslie Hotson has recently rediscovered it for some of us brings
back the eyes. For we suddenly see that it was not, as it has
become, a box for puppets (clever ones, to be sure), a di-version,
but, as the theatre of Ze-ami and the theatre of Eschylus was, a
place of complete occasion, a theatre FOR experience.

I like also, and Zukofsky, in character, brings it out through
nice comparisons, not at all invidious, the toughness of Shakespeare's mind, always at the same time graceful, but firmly rooted
in experience:

> *Pericles.* Nor come we to add sorrow to your tears,
> But to relieve them of their heavy load . . .
> We do not look for reverence but for love. . . .
> *(I, iv., 90 ff.)*

151

And Samuel Johnson, as Zukofsky enters, points out that vivacity that only a spirit that retains zest uncannily can project, in Shakespeare:

> . . . he always makes us anxious for the event. . . .
>
> . . . he has seen with his own eyes . . . he gives the image which he receives, not weakened or distorted by the intervention of any other mind; the ignorant feel his representations to be just, and the learned see that they are compleat. . . .
>
> When he describes anything, you more than see it, you feel it too. . . .

Or (it is always "or" with such a con-text): as Christopher Smart in his *Jubilate Agno* says of the first poet:

> For he played upon the harp in the spirit by breathing
>   upon the strings.

Zukofsky finds Shakespeare's eyes in France, of course, as well as everywhere else the heart has found out speech. So that Voltaire writes to his Madame du Deffand:

> . . . Forgive me, madam, for speaking to you of a pleasure enjoyed through the eyes: you only know the pleasures of the soul. . . . You replace the passions by philosophy, a poor substitute: while I replace them with the tender and respectful attachment I have always felt for you.

There may be too much residual of a feeling of the lace cuff in these handsome words, but there's an edge too of aged eyes. More taking and touching is this burst from Flaubert:

> . . . When I read Shakespeare . . . I am an *eye*. . . . Long ago . . . speaking of the joy caused by the reading of the great poets I said: "I often felt that the enthusiasm they kindled made me their equal and raised me to a level with themselves." . . . stop being hurt because I speak to you about Shakespeare instead of about myself. It's just that he seems to me more interesting . . . if you put the sun inside your trousers, all you do is burn your trousers and wet the sun. This is what happened to (Musset). Nerves,

magnetism: for him poetry is those things. Actually, it is something less turbulent. If sensitive nerves were the only requirement of a poet, I should be superior to Shakespeare and to Homer, whom I picture as a not very nervous individual. Such confusion is blasphemy.

And so, on into American letters, words, eyes.

I'll presume on Z's excellence of quotation from Edwards, Poe and Thoreau and some surprises, to add the dainty to endearing to profound note of Emily Dickinson whom he leaves quite alone, for she has curious eyes too and never the heart not minded in them. When she receives a letter from a friend who tries to kill two birds with one stone, the other bird being Lavinia, naturally, Emily scolds:

Sister—a mutual plum is not a plum. I was too respectful to take the pulp and do not like the stone.

Dear Friend,
      . . . Do you look out tonight? The moon rides . . . I don't think we shall ever be merry again—you are ill so long. When did the dark happen? I skipped a page tonight, because I come so often, now, I might have tired you. *That* page is fullest, though. . . .

Dear Mary,—
      The last April that father lived, lived I mean below, there were several snowstorms, and the birds were so frightened and cold, they sat by the kitchen door. Father went to the barn in his slippers and came back with a breakfast of grain for each, and his himself while he scattered it, lest it embarrass them. . . .

How Hamlet-like Emily is here, how Shakespeare. For she eavesdrops the eavesdropper, not to embarrass *him*—yet love remembers in the eyes and in the words that see so far, direction is lost.

      . . . Affection is like bread, unnoticed till we starve, and then we dream of it, and sing of it, and paint it, when every urchin in the street has more than he can eat. We turn older with the years, but newer every day. . . .

. . . I am happy to be your scholar, and will deserve the kindness I cannot repay. . . .

. . . While Shakespeare remains, literature is firm. . . .

. . . The ear is the last face. We hear after we see, which to tell you first is still my destiny. . . .

To turn the account slightly back in historical time and forward into our critical temperature no one works like Melville, that horse, does, as Zukofsky sees:

But I was talking about the "Whale" . . . I'm going . . . to finish him up in some fashion or other. What's the use of elaborating what, in its very essence, is so shortlived as a modern book? Though I wrote the Gospels in this century I should die in the gutter. . . .

It is a frightful poetical creed that the cultivation of the brain eats out the heart. But it's my *prose* opinion that in most cases, in those men who have fine brains and work them well, the heart extends down to the hams. And though you smoke them with the fire of tribulation, yet, like veritable hams, the head only gives the richer and better flavor. I stand for the heart. To the dogs with the head! I had rather be a fool with a heart, than Jupiter Olympus with his head.

LZ naturally finds his text in *Lear*, as Melville himself did:

Lear. Hysterica passio, down . . . / The element's below!

Fool. All that followed their noses are led by their eyes but blind men . . . not a nose among twenty but can smell him that's stinking. Let go thy hold when a great wheel runs down a hill, lest it break thy neck with following. . . .

154

Each thing obtains the other at its own expense, becomes the other. Extremes of black and white suggest basics. As though one went to source by stripping down to cries. The push through is, however, in how color lives within the black and white of it (how much color there is in an Eisenstein film and how little in *Ben-Hur*), how the eye, drawn by the quiet of this connection, gets down into things (knee-deep in prayer), whereby it sees and dwells within a world it is always out amidst.

In relation to this, other eyes may be called to witness differences: first, a Western poet's in the face of Chinese painting and then a Japanese poet's as his poetry projects it.

Laurence Binyon writes (*The Spirit of Man in Asian Art*): "With Chinese, space often becomes the protagonist in the design. It is not final peace, but itself an activity flowing out from the picture into our minds, and drawing us into a rarer atmosphere. It is tranquilizing, but even more so, it is exhilarating."

And, in fact, in his book *Hua Ch'uan* or *The Net of Painting*, Ta Chung-k'uang writes:

> White vacancy is *yang,* or light; solid ink wash is
> *yin,* or darkness. . . .

All of this may sound rather mystical not to say hazy, but what is felt is not, though it may not be of an explicable or wholly extricable nature.

When Basho on his long walk recorded in the *Oku-no-hoso-michi* on the evening of the Tanabata (Star) Festival (a midsummer night) looks at the island of exiles (Sado) on the Japan Sea coast, the words he has perpetuated for eyes:

ara-umi-ya	wild seas (ya
Sado-ni yokoto	to Sado shoring up
ama-no-gawa	the River of Heaven

where "the River of Heaven" is usually rendered, less vividly here, by our "Milky Way," the thought feeling is clearly not one of "annihilation" and it registers a difference not only of eyes (think how Emily Dickinson's "Wild seas!" erupt into personal passion) but of the heart's intelligence intricate in them. For Basho looking out over a turbulent sea towards the evening's horizon sees that sad island as only the highest wave of that moment bringing the eye to the sky with its stream of stars, from the vastity and confusion of the nearer noisier sea to the very pitch of isolation and returning not by sea but by see! by the artery of heaven's stars, to the shore made more immensely silent, lost and celebrant in breath's breathlessness.

And Emily's cry finds Basho eyes when she finally says: "Not what the stars have done, but what they are to do, is what detains the sky. . . ."

Zukofsky sees through Shakespeare's scales and Henry Adams' *Education*, America's blindnesses (Emerson and Whitman too had seen much that even De Tocqueville hadnt):

> The typical American man had his hand on a lever and his eye on a curve in the road. . . . He could not run his machine and a woman too. . . . From the male, she could look for no help; his instinct of power was blind. . . .
>
> No one means all he says, and yet very few say all they mean, for words are slippery and thought is viscous . . . since Bacon and Newton, English thought had gone on impatiently protesting that no one must try to know the unknowable at the same time that every one went on thinking about it. . . .

And Henry James, leading one on into Shakespeare's mind:

> . . . He leads us into his own mind, his own vision of things: that's the only place into which the poet *can* lead us. . . .

It brings us at least

> —they had eyes . . .
> —and saw,
> saw with their proper eyes. . . .

But it is difficult in America for the quiet note to be heard and the value of sheer noise is inflated. Quietness is taken as complacency or smugness or dulness or lord knows what, as though each man has not to suffer what he lives, or as though there were some special grace in imposing one's own misery on others and making it pay off too as "art."

Nowhere is tranquillity more distrusted and yet precisely America invents and requires its tranquillizers. It will accept drugs, or any gimmick, for its nerves, but will not *live* its day in peace. The image of battle, of murder, obtains the assent and fervor of the marketplace and the assent and fervor of the religious sages in the West (and it moves East as well now with the flow of the "modern" and "progress"). Ecstasy, if many had their way, would be as much a drugstore commodity (convenience) and week-end entertainment as, say, sexual freedom.

The "Who am I?" lament, the great American intellectual burden, serves as a saleable anguish; anything does that does not need the care, say, evidenced in each word's behavior and sense in this very book and in each note's of its companion volume, caring for what others have *cared* to say with due order, out of love toward that continuing possibility.

The commitment is not one that asks a gavel or a lectern; it seeks us every day and every moment thereof, invokes us utterly, married or single (or should I say "*and* single"?), old or young (or should I say "*and* young"?), in ill health or not (or should I say "dying"?).

All these words that Zukofsky has found for Shakespeare seem to have been found *in* Shakespeare. Everything brings us back to where we are, to see through words that sing something clearer of what we are. The author of

If love exists, why remember it?

proves as he moves to *Definition* (finally, to begin there), that he is ready to speak with his "son" in terms of Shakescene's very own eyes' words.

4

Definition provides for the questioning reader, who comes with love, whatever answers are necessary for "bothering." It is father to son in kindness, in candid con-versation: a dialogue on poetry, often in poetry, mostly Shakespeare's.

The author answers the son's wanting to know more of what love is Shakespeare's, reiterating:

... *love is to reason as the eyes are to the mind;* or
says it (the Works) so that *means* equal *extremes:*

157

when reason judges with eyes, love and mind are
one. . . .

Without love's eyes art sees no sensible life . . .
"everything must grow out of the subject and there
must be nothing new." . . . the sun's art recurs in
the lover's art; the sky's eye acts in lovers' eyes.
Unseen (the sun) and closed (the eyes) they are for
only humming ears.

When the son asks, more boldly than the reader can: "Isn't
anybody's reading of Shakespeare as good as yours?" the father
answers simply: "Maybe better. But if *your* taste is only yours,
and *mine* only mine, why bother to look or to read Shakespeare
together? Where is his or Shakespeare's art?"

The son, nobody's fool, retorts: "In everybody. Yet . . . how
deep can you wade? . . . Why do you cite endlessly, and presume
to cover 'continents,' sidetracking to analogies which I've heard
you say you have no taste for, you whom scholars and strays do
not attract?"

And the father: "For once—so the definition of love in
Shakespeare may flourish. . . ."

> . . . Flourish
> By love's sweet lights and sing *in them I flourish*. . . .

Citations are heaped up at the altar of this definition. For
myself I'd see it in the dimension of generations (generosities), of
father and son, father to son, son to father, a transmission.

For love exists in only such eyes as see through those of the
dead who live in us, our persistence, and the dying:

> For all inwreathed in me
> That make my love
> Your fiddle,
> to some imagined music,
> When it shall be your own
> In the world, thru some sense of the bow alone
> Shall tell the strings
> Their Great World quietly—
> In the time I owe the world nothing—
>   What in you
> Of my father who owed a Source
>   Or his little fish

158

Of when I walked with him,
With you or with Celia, a night
Or with the winds
Say what their wonders with cities are
With seas in arms of landscape, a thought or a hand
Slowing that I do not see death
When an air seems too much in the air:
My time will run me
I am not all of my time
No one is all of it. . . .

or earlier in *"A"-12*, that beauty of twentieth century poetry,

. . . no one cares about anything he does not love
And love is pleasure that dwells on its cause. . . .

So it is that the Freudian commonplace that does not see in Sophocles' *Oedipus* what is in the words and at the heart of that experience "sublimates" its own analytical desire into the jargon of the "Oedipus complex" and would instil the idea that son "naturally" contends with father for mother. It is pat, of course, for Freud and company to labor the point by saying it's all a "cover-up," but that's the endless round of peeling the onion for the emptiness that centers it. Eyes that care will not "bite" or "snap." Sure, there are "troubles" and men do love their trammels, weaving plies of complexities and complexes, a mesh of guilts and sins or hierarchic fault, and it may be "human," but one doesnt feel hatred in Sophocles *or* father against son. No more than one feels revolt, natural or otherwise, in the relations that obtain between Odysseus and Telemachus, between Aeneas and his father or his son, between Zukofsky grandfather, father and son, between Shakespeare father and son.

The Hasidic lore, as Buber transmits it, is virtually all father and son. Freud looks sick when one sees through these eyes:

Rabbi Pinhas used to say: "What you pursue, you
don't get. But what you allow to grow slowly in its
own way, comes to you. Cut open a big fish, and in
its belly you will find the little fish lying head down."

(A nice transformation in kind from
the Indian political proverb of big fish
swallowing little.)

159

It is told:

When Rabbi Shelomo drank tea or coffee, it was his custom to take a piece of sugar and hold it in his hand the entire time he was drinking. Once his son asked him: "Father, why do you do that? If you need sugar, put it in your mouth, but if you do not need it, why hold it in your hand!"

When he had emptied his cup, the rabbi gave the piece of sugar he had been holding to his son and said: "Taste it." The son put it in his mouth and was very much astonished, for there was no sweetness at all left in it. Later, when the son told this story, he said: "A man, in whom everything is unified, can taste with his hand, as if with his tongue."

And finally, just this (not for analysis but for clear feeling, the only health):

Each year, the maggid of Koznitz visited his father's grave in the city of Apt. On one such occasion, the heads of the community came to him to ask him to preach in the great House of Prayer on the sabbath, as he had done the year before. "Is there any reason to believe," he said, "that I accomplished anything with my last year's sermon?" The men left in dismay, and the entire community was stricken with grief. A crowd collected in front of the maggid's inn. All stood silent with bowed heads. But then a man, a craftsman, came forward, went into the maggid's room, and said to him: "You claim that you did not accomplish anything with the sermon you preached last year. You did accomplish something as far as I am concerned. For at that time I heard from your lips the words that every son of Israel must do as it says in the Scriptures: 'I have set the Lord always before me.' Ever since then I see the name of the Lord before me, like black fire on white fire."

"If that is the case," said the maggid, "I shall go and preach a sermon."

Is it inapt, again, to note that Shakespeare found time in all his labors to secure his father a desired coat-of-arms and found in

Hamlet somewhat of his dead son Hamnet's name? The care that is in the work is the profoundest witness of the care that was in the life, for it lives still as such.

Where the love, indeed, in Shakespeare's eyes flourishes most and makes us all sons of his sun is in the very theatre of his words. No word, at best, fails to happen, fails to tell as it makes event, "shapes up" as it shapes out.

Consider *Hamlet*. I take it, since likely most known. Wallace Stevens, presumably reminiscing, recalls:

> Long ago, Sarah Bernhardt was playing Hamlet. When she came to the soliloquy "To be or not to be," she half turned her back on the audience and slowly weaving one hand in a small circle above her head and regarding it, she said, with deliberation and as from the depths of an hallucination:
> *D'être ou ne pas d'être, c'est là la question.* . . .
> and one followed her, lost in the intricate metamorphosis of thoughts that passed through the mind with a gallantry, an accuracy of abundance, a crowding and pressing of direction, which, for thoughts that were both borrowed and confused, cancelled the borrowing and obliterated the confusion.

So that there is a clarity that one spectator anyhow saw in what one actor saw in what Hamlet saw of what Shakespeare saw in him or through him, so that we are, if anyone is, the ghost of whatever spirit still abides in and holds converse with this world and courts us to the edge.

But one should also see that Shakespeare himself has Hamlet *playing* Hamlet confuse us so that, before we know it, we are seeing ourselves through those eyes, so that when he says at last "Now I am alone," and the motion in the words says, sees us to the heart, that the *am* eyes *alone,* each of us is then alone, Hamlet to the core. No director does Shakespeare, but each of us performers at his pitch. Nor do stage directions lack; the text embodies them. The scene is always in the words and fully presented so. Everything acts. Shakespeare sees *to* center because he sees *from* center. The words strike home. We know where we are, there, here, for the words are *telling*.

O, what a rogue and peasant slave am I!

And now the emphasis has turned upon itself, from *am* to *I*! How many readers see as well as the words see?

Is it not monstrous that this player here

(how palpable Shakespeare keeps event: these are not symbols, counters, or myths that we encounter: nor does he forget where he is, where we are, what is going on and has transpired in this theatre of eyes)

But in a fiction, in a dream of passion,
Could force his soul to his own conceit
That from her working all his visage wanned,
Tears in his eyes, distraction in his aspect,
A broken voice, and his whole function suiting
With forms to his conceit; and all for nothing!

(The mousetrap being set to catch a king's conscience catches also that of the coward self that sicklies resolution. And now he does not know, wonders if, like all play, it comes to nothing, or the general truth.) And now the conscience of man makes free:

For Hecuba!
What's Hecuba to him, or he to Hecuba,
That he should weep for her? what would he do,
Had he the motive and the cue for passion
That I have?

The way the words move and break, not merely to the look on a page but in the moving air of utterance, tells the sigh that tells this question's end. The words *perform:* they eye us and the theatre.

He would drown the stage in tears
And cleave the general ear with horrid speech,
Make mad the guilty and appal the free,
Confound the ignorant, and amaze indeed
The very faculties of eyes and ears. . . .

Here the flood of rhetoric needs no damming; it needs spate for finding its proper aim and anger, self-abuse, to give it ample ground through the sound of it. He would warrant melodrama, since acting is the scope allowed him, such as he abuses Ophelia with, before he finds the painful calm to teach his scholar-actors the rationale of their trade.

162

How this man (and who is Hamlet, who is man, so much of each other's history has each become?) immediately has words to his intent is marvellous to behold. One knows, feels, experience has eyes and sees from the heart when the words do too.

The mind itself as it eyes itself assumes a shape, not pleasing perhaps, but undeniable and shaking.

Or how to follow through, as Shakespeare inevitably does, seeing and seizing upon phrases, clutches, of words, and single words, to build his scenes upon and with, or draw them more dearly to momentum. How "looks" prevail in *Hamlet* and "fair" becomes as foul as in *Macbeth.* How "heaven" stands excuse for love's demise, love's delay. The word "forget" itself is constantly remembered.

So rich does Shakespeare as Zukofsky read that, as at a Noh performance truly rendered, one exclaims (who sees)—even, or most, at pauses: Whoa there! Not so fast! Dont *do* so much! I cant keep up! For everything matters: nothing needs feel itself neglected (the attender is fully attended): everything is always "in play," at stake. Every word is a cast of the dice. Every word, the last word.

Editors and theorists, beware! This is no place for them. This is a world poetry alone experiences. Its practise is its theory and texts beg no improvement at the hands of "ingenious" editors.

Who sees as much as well as Zukofsky sees, sees much well indeed.

> *When icicles hang by the wall:* the Mozartian song
> of it, generous, gentle, humble to listen to, that
> merry note makes as if to see into lovers' ears—some
> forecast of the seasonable in any time of year in the
> country of Watteau painting and Boucher textile
> print: more France than its history.

What can one say finally except not to say finally, in one's own way, the same experience, of varying particular, out of love, toward quietness. To speak silence in its own tongue. *Wovon man nicht sprechen kann, darüber muss man schweigen.*

Love sees, No tongue! All eyes!

All textual arguments that Zukofsky scores only come to the same theme: "Let the writer be the *definition." Pericles,* which

163

even the latest editors reject as wholly Shakespeare's, though there
is *no* sound evidence against the ascription, finds its justice in the
canon undisputed and indisputable in the theme that Zukofsky
serves in all of Shakespeare's Works. The words tell.

5

The alphabet (now at page 342) enters its final phase of dance
and speeds up. The sections are notably shorter and shorter, but
the theme, as it is fractioned into particular issues: light and
sources and sounds, glows more constant:

> . . . The flame cannot rise save from some body. In
> the flame are two lights: one white and luminous,
> the other black or blue. . . . This is the secret of the
> sacrifice. The ascending smoke kindles the blue light
> which then attaches itself to the white, so that the
> whole candle is completely alight . . . the blue light
> cleaving to the white and consuming fat and flesh of
> burnt-offering beneath it, for it does not consume
> what is beneath it save when it ascends and attaches
> itself to the white light. Then there is peace in all
> worlds and the whole forms a unity.
>
> <div align="right">(<i>Zohar, I, 50b-51b</i>)</div>

By these lights, this light, that joins all continents and every
definition that renders man, in "Ember Eves" have we moved
towards conclusion, or that more open opening that draws our fire.
A clarity of moment it is that says:

> All that I have to say, is to tell you, that the Lan-
> thorne is the Moone; I, the man in the Moone; this
> thorne bush, my thorne bush; and this dog, my dog.

I see a voice.

It is a major beauty in this book, as the author marshals texts
and sounds and intelligences that all the voices flow into one voice
and that one of such incredible particularity and excellence that one
is like to ask, Who is this guy, Homer-Aristotle-Aquinas-Shake-
speare-Spinoza-Wittgenstein-Zukofsky? It isnt at all unlike the

164

Mediterraneans with their fondness for the long baptismal name invoking every worthy ancestor (heritage is heir) towards one name to walk and breathe and see again its way towards death and another.

"Forgotten" is remembered: Zukofsky sees clowns "smiling together over the same lines" Shakespeare provides as fuel for them. The long coal and the brief body and the light that comes from both, to warm and illuminate, illustrious: who has time to be lonely who gives his time to others? Love shares only timelessness in moment and does not yield its care to having to know that, dwells within occasion simply.

> Hang there like fruit, my soul,
> Till the tree die.
> > (*Cymbeline*, V, v. 261)

Empedocles: *Frag. 109:*

> By the earth, water, air in us we know earth, water,
> divine air; by our fire, the consuming fire; love by
> love, and hate by cursed hate.

As Hamlet to Horatio, Zukofsky to Shakespeare through this very book where they join Works, as I recall in the Uffizi where I used to wander for months several times a week and always paused before a late self-portrait of Rembrandt and found myself conversing with him there and thought, felt, saw, that if he could retain so much love towards an unknown me, through all too obvious suffering and painstakingness, I had a friend to keep me all my life alive. And so Zukofsky touches in Democritus, *Frag. 99,* a Greek accord:

> No one deserves to live who has not at least one good
> friend.

And the useful corollary of *Frag. 119:*

> Men idolize luck as an excuse for their thoughtless-
> ness. Luck seldom crosses swords with wisdom. Most
> things in life wit and attentive eyes set right.

Or how *Hamlet* concludes.

Is there anyone "in the house" who has lived many years intelligently who has not at some time realized on seeing words of this order: But how *much* has been experienced and well-expressed already! What is the *progress* in mankind we think to pride ourselves on all these centuries since? How much better can we see than these have seen? And how slow, in fact, we are to see what they *have* seen and committed to us!

Honor is the unaspirated H that Zukofsky gets at, spelled out in *"A"-11,*

> Honor, song, sang the blest is delight knowing
> We overcome ills by love. Hurt, song, nourish
> Eyes, think most of whom you hurt. . . .
>
> Honor

> His voice in me, the river's turn that finds the
> Grace in you, four notes first too full for talk, leaf
> Lighting stem, stems bound to the branch that binds the
> Tree, and then as from the same root we talk, leaf
> After leaf of your mind's music, page, walk leaf
> Over leaf of this thought, sounding
> His happiness: song sounding
> The grace that comes from knowing
> Things, her love our own showing
> Her love in all her honor.

The unaspirated H aspirates to "happiness." He merely "talks": no, not when he sings. "Read," as the son says, for whom it was written, in *"A"-12,* "what it says."

As for sources ("larnin' "), a Shakespeare that knew his Florio Montaigne and North Plutarch would have already had experienced much Greek and Latin and not much less English, given the vitality of the Tudor tongue even untutored. London was a world of intense reach then and "new" with its possibility too, so that the daily life Shakespeare was clearly so involved in was most fertile ground. Everything, if you like, was "going" for him and he, all open, went for it. The connections that the author makes, then, between Shakespeare's words and those of the classical past are only what we would expect, though the pleasure of Shakespeare's tongue savoring and sounding the ancients' increases with the telling.

The section on music ("Musicks Letters") would want entire quote to do it justice, and how much any poet or good reader can come up with here is all diamond.

The impression Shakespeare's text leaves a reader who is inclined to feel that one book judges and is judged by all other books is a comment on music thru history. On the other hand, the text also conveys the impression that whatever Shakespeare's dramatis personae have to say about good music their analysis has, as self-proof, less harmony to offer than a song: for a song when heard by inexplainable proof of its own has that sense of the *substantial* known rather like the seeing of the eye than the idiom of the brain. Affected by both impressions the reader whose craft is not music thinks of the violinist keeping the sound together by his orderly fingering at which he looks while playing—his eyes exercised to effortless fleetness; but he limits his looking as he listens not to outrun tangibly the critically fleeting visible order, so that no wrong twisting of fingers can effect a frightened look that the sound may not come clear. . . .

. . . if the musician's ear does not love its song as the lover's eyes love their sight, he will not know it as "a type of human nature to which we may look." One extreme of hearing for him may be—tho that will almost not be his nature's word—"silence."

I wonder at current notions of "sublimation," thinking, say, of Bach, who fathered so many many children, was never not, it seems, at music, writing, teaching, playing, moving around, loving his family. As a friend who is also an artist (which means most man) exactly remarks, But love feeds into the work and leads from the work also back, renewed, to the love. Who needs any sublime excuse?

Even the script of a Bach score, as he wrote it, plays music for eyes: the quill that in a sweep gathers a swoop of notes, the clarity with which the notes are spaced and shaped and placed on the page and joined, is instrumental to one's sense of what one has heard of his music or ever will. Or as Zukofsky repeats of what *he* has heard, as if to corroborate what I have seen and felt:

Bach's feet it is said danced his fugue at the organ.

N: "I know the man as well as yourself."

The "master of music, Pericles (whose name means *risk*)"
Zukofsky goes on to say, describing his "lot" is "to embrace
Thaisa in time after the life she gave birth to (Marina) lives to
make his. It is then he hears the music of the spheres. For truth
being positive can never be confirmed enough, tho doubt—in
which no positive is granted—sleeps deprived. Yet as the master of
music sleeps to be restored under rarest sounds of the round above
him, the wisest or most loving beholder cannot say whether his
importance is joy or sorrow."

Under "Wonder" Zukofsky lets Theseus play Bottom for
him and, as it happens, for me:

> No epilogue, I pray you; for your play needs no
> excuse. Never excuse. . . .

It is a world to see.

And so Z, closing the spelling out, as signature: the z of a
wizard and one true, the z of the hum on OM (as the Cockney
might say: *'om* is where the *'art* is), beyond the hiss of any ess, or
bottomless ass. So that the last letter makes the first (*"A"*) make
sense.

The book is done, though the index has a way at the end of
seeing us back again and again.

The music alone remains. As the son puts it, in his own
voice:

> All the instruments have the words.

Postscript: *Not* in epilogue, but as "post" script, for Zukofsky
in a letter just reaching me as this ends says (as so
beautiful a make as "It Was" had long since confirmed) of the footnote on p. 37 *Bottom* ("Celia
Thaew's *Pericles* an opera to all the words of the
play by William Shakespeare—the one excuse for all
that follows in this part."):

> ". . . And yes I mean that footnote . . . & will mean it
> more and more as the world understands less & less
> how much I mean it."

168

Or how biographers that find every love for Shakespeare but his own that he kept constantly going back to Stratford for and to which he retired (the "second-best bed" always being that of the host, the "first-best" belonging to the guest, as a poet's words to his guests) hate to admit that lovely simplicity.

No one can make poetry who doesnt live it every day.

Kyoto
August-September 1963

Printed January 1977 in Santa Barbara & Ann Arbor
for the Black Sparrow Press by Mackintosh and Young
& Edwards Brothers Inc. Design by Barbara Martin.
This edition is published in paper wrappers; there are
500 hardcover trade copies; 200 hardcover copies
are numbered & signed by the author; & 50 numbered
copies have been handbound in boards by Earle Gray,
each containing an original holograph poem by Cid Corman.

Photo: John Levy

Cid Corman was born in Boston in 1924. He was educated at
Boston Latin School and Tufts College. He did postgraduate work
at the University of Michigan (where he won the Hopwood Award
in 1947), the University of North Carolina, and the Sorbonne. In
1951 he founded *Origin: a quarterly for the creative,* which has
now gone through three series. (Corman's anthology, *The Gist of
Origin,* has recently been published by Grossman.) Since 1954 he
has lived mostly in Europe and Japan, and still runs Origin Press
from his home in Kyoto, where he and his wife also operate an ice
cream shop.

Cid Corman has published more than sixty books, many from
small presses. Next year Black Sparrow will bring out the second
volume of his literary essays, *At Their Word,* and a collection of
poems, *Root Song.*